CONVERSATIONS *on* CHRISTIAN FEMINISM

Speaking Heart to Heart

Elaine Storkey

and

Margaret Hebblethwaite

Fount
An Imprint of HarperCollinsPublishers

Fount is an Imprint of
HarperCollins*Religious*
Part of HarperCollins*Publishers*
77–85 Fulham Palace Road, London W6 8JB

First published in Great Britain in 1999 by Fount

1 3 5 7 9 10 8 6 4 2

Elaine Storkey and Margaret Hebblethwaite assert the
moral right to be identified as the authors of this work

A catalogue record for this book
is available from the British Library

ISBN 000 627879 5

Printed and bound in Great Britain by
Caledonian International Book Manufacturing Ltd, Glasgow

CONVERSATIONS *on* CHRISTIAN FEMINISM

CONTENTS

INTRODUCTION

This is not the usual kind of book, but a new idiom. It is not a written book pretending to be a conversation, but a real conversation – in fact, sixteen real conversations – which we have taped and edited and put on to the printed page. Why? Because it is both more interesting and more revealing to listen in to a living conversation than to read a dead slab of text. And this is particularly true when the speakers are genuinely searching together and bouncing ideas off each other.

Feminist theology is not a fixed, established discipline with all the answers intact. It is a new subject, a pioneering venture into territory that is covered with brambles and littered with potholes. So we have allowed the reader to share in our search, and to sense when we are enthusiastic or when we are frustrated, when we are angry or when we are puzzled, when we are pained or when we are excited.

We both believe profoundly that traditional Christian faith must be united with contemporary insights on the equality of women, for the health of both. We have talked through the issues of feminist theology right across the board, in a way that will make the book a useful introduction to the subject for non-theologians, as well as a contribution to the ongoing debates of theologians. We do not have all the answers, but we have a sense of today's questions and we also have some fairly strong convictions.

All the way through we have shown how our own experiences have shaped our thinking. We may come from quite opposite church backgrounds but we have much in common. We are both laywomen, wives and mothers, who work in the field of Christian communication. And as we have talked our way through this book, we have become great friends.

One

BECOMING A FEMINIST

MARGARET: How did you become a feminist, Elaine?

ELAINE: I was quite slow in waking up to feminism. I had been brought up in the north of England as an academic succeeder in a family where my parents greatly valued education. My brother, sister and I – they are both younger than myself – were all encouraged to work hard at grammar school. And I enjoyed study: I loved literature, language analysis, history – everything that children of my age in our area didn't normally like. Then, when I was sixteen I had a conversion experience which changed my life. I've been a committed Christian ever since.

I threw myself into everything, became head girl of the local grammar school, went to university, did rather well – was president of the Philosophical Society, climbed with the mountaineering group, played hockey and lacrosse, joined the Christian Union, and so on. Feminism simply didn't feature on my agenda, because from sixth form onwards I was surrounded by women who were smart and academically minded, and no one thought of themselves as in any sense second class.

But what I hadn't realized was that I had modelled myself on men since my earliest years without even recognizing it. Although my close friends were all women, my mentors were all men. I was in a mixed school with a headmaster I thought fantastic: he was a playwright, an academic, a lawyer and a great fan of George Herbert and C.S. Lewis. He was very influential with the sixth form, and I admired his ideas. At university in Wales there was an all-male faculty in philosophy, and my own thinking was greatly influenced by them. I went off to Canada where I was a graduate student in philosophy, and the same again: the lecturers were all men.

I formulated the expectation that although my close women friends were intellectually aware, most women were not, and they weren't expected to do the thinking. At graduate school I would usually be in all-male company because I was the only woman on my courses. When we visited the home of one of the graduates (most of them were married) I would inevitably be in the lounge with the men, discussing the great issues of God, life, the universe and the Dutch philosopher Hermann Dooyeweerd, while the women would be busying around in the kitchen getting food to feed us. It never occurred to me to be in the kitchen with the women, it seemed perfectly natural in the lounge with my pipe-smoking colleagues, thinking great thoughts!

So, unconsciously, I had absorbed much inherent sexism without ever thinking it through. I thought like a man. And when people told me, 'You think like a man,' I would take it as a vague compliment – it didn't matter one way or the other. I would also fight tooth and nail in an argument to win; I wouldn't let anything get past me.

It really wasn't until after I was married that I started to think of myself in a different way. Feminism hadn't played any conscious part in my choice of a spouse. The main criterion was that he must be a Christian. But I knew he would have to be someone I could respect intellectually, and who would respect me in the same way. And that's been true. After I had children my whole outlook changed. When our first child was a baby, my husband Alan worked at home and we both worked on projects and childcare together. This lasted for three years. But six months after we had our second son we broke that pattern. We moved areas; Alan went out to work in a college and I stayed at home with two small children. That was an enormous shock.

For the first time in my life I became one of these 'other' women – not an academic woman in languid company, but a woman with children and housework and an interminable list of things to get through. It completely threw me. I used to phone up other mothers and ask, 'What do you do all day?' They would say, 'Well, we do the housework.' And I would say, 'Well, I've done the housework. What do you do next?' And they would reply, 'You can't have done the housework, it takes all day to do the housework.'

I just didn't have any way of latching into normal women's lives. It was extraordinary, really. I mean, I had the experience of my childhood in Ossett with many women in my family, and I knew women's stories, and had an enormous empathy towards women. But it was relearning a whole language of being a woman.

So, I went to my local FE college and said, 'Could I run an evening class for women who are like I am, largely housebound?' They agreed and it became enormously successful. Husbands babysat and women came out to study. That was really the beginning of a feminist journey for me. My students were mostly local people who had little formal education, and I taught them sociology at O level and A level. One or two even went on to university. When I left, one of my former students, who had started with me at A level, took on my job.

It wasn't until many years after my student days that I was able to reflect on my own background and recognize the attitudes I had imbibed and repent of them because they were so demeaning towards women. Now I find women's company much more exciting than most men's.

MARGARET: That's surprisingly similar in many ways to me, although the details are different.

I grew up with one brother, a mother and a father. My father was more intellectual than my mother. Right from my childhood I knew that boys' schools were better than girls' schools, and I thought that monks were better than nuns – more interesting and better educated. Men had jobs, women did housework.

So my aim was to be an honorary man, or an honorary boy. So, looking back, I can see that I internalized discrimination. I myself was sexist in that I thought men were better than women. I wanted to belong to the men's club and to the extent that I could, I would.

When I was a student, I heard about women's lib – this was still in the days of burning bras. I really couldn't understand what it was about and I thought, 'This is absurd, women today are not oppressed. They used to be, of course.'

After university – where I studied theology and philosophy, but theology was my real thing always – I became involved in a church run by a male religious order, and I was very aware of being part of the struggle of laity against clericalism. I did feel oppressed then, not because I was a woman but because I was a layperson.

If you belonged to the particular club of this religious order then you were regarded as the expert in whatever you happened to be interested in. Everyone else was just the person in the pew who had to sit and listen. You could watch this when people joined the community: someone who had been nobody before would be asked to give talks the moment he became a novice. And I resented this very much.

Now this didn't push me towards being feminist. It actually had rather the opposite effect, because I noticed that the religious order was very pro women's theology, but I felt they were using this as a tool to manipulate their own superior position. They were able to say to women: 'Ah, if you want to do theology you should join the women's theology group.' But everyone knew that the serious theological work was coming out of their little group, which they didn't let you belong to. They were the ones who taught and preached, and being a woman you were automatically classed as a kind of amateur.

The more they said they to me: 'Margaret, I think you would be happier if you joined the women's theology group,' the more I felt that these male clerics were trying to keep me off their patch, and the more I detested this group and regarded women's theology as something second best. It took quite a while for that to break down.

My other reason for being a bit anti feminist theology was that in the early days it was rather militant and negative. I could agree 100 per cent with the aim of bringing in the women's dimension: it is so obvious that the whole of history has been slanted towards men. I applauded that aim, but I didn't like the way they did it. Feminist theology at that date seemed to be identified with the particular approach of attacking what was called patriarchy. That irritated me, the talk of patriarchy. I found the whole language abstract and pretentious, as though trying to play the men's game without having their skills.

ELAINE: How did that change?

MARGARET: It began to change after I wrote *Motherhood and God* (Geoffrey Chapman, 1984). We were in Rome for two years, and I went to the Gregorian University. I was in a spirituality group of a hundred people, and we were asked to write an essay on 'A Stage in my Personal Pilgrimage', which is not the sort of essay subject you are given at Oxford.

I was a bit scornful of it, and I thought I would just toss it off. But at the same time I thought, 'What can I do, in a class of a hundred people, that is going to be different from everyone else?' There were other women in the group but they were all nuns, so I thought I would write about having babies: no one else could touch me on that.

To do that properly it was evident to me immediately that I should call God 'she' and explore the image of God as mother. In those days this was very new. I had no doubts about its legitimacy but it was something that hadn't really been done before. So I wrote the essay very quickly, and when you write personal things quickly often they work out well because they just flow out of you. I thought, 'Gosh, I'm really on to something.' So I came back to England and developed it into a book.

What surprised me was that after the book came out, Christian feminists began to own me. I didn't realize I was doing feminist theology, and I didn't at first know how to react to the invitations to speak. But quite soon I warmed up and realized that feminist theology was broader and more open than I had thought, and that you didn't have to do it in a militant, negative way. You could also do it in a way that tried to enrich our understanding of God, and say positive things.

Not that my book was universally liked by feminists. There were some who felt they already had enough of being stereotyped into the category of mothers, and then there were women who were single or childless and said, 'I felt bad enough beforehand, now I feel doubly excluded.' But I appreciated particularly letters from men or from nuns – from people who hadn't had this experience but could say, 'This is an important insight for all of us.'

Since then I have been to an increasing number of women's 'do's. The first time I went to a women-only meeting was in Brussels in 1987, for a Catholic colloquium on 'Women in the Church and in Society', with women from all over the world preparing for the Synod on the Laity in Rome that year. And I found to my surprise that I liked it being women only. I had thought I wouldn't, and in fact I did.

And then there were other experiences. There was a big ecumenical congress called Celebrating Christian Women in Liverpool in 1988, and that was very good indeed. It was women's way of doing things: we did circle dancing and on the first evening we blessed and handed round a glass of water. I thought this was so funny – just imagine a group of men doing that!

Then we had little groups called oasis circles. The woman who was co-ordinating my group ended the first evening by saying, 'Let's say the Lord's Prayer,' assuming this was one prayer that united women of all denominations, but we all suddenly became aware that one woman was screwed up and tense, and eventually with great pain she got out the words, 'Are we going to pray like this on other evenings? Because if so I had better not come.' That was my first face-to-face experience of how the Our Father can be a stumbling block.

I was talking of militancy, which originally I didn't like, but at that conference I took a step into militancy myself. There was a great solidarity among the women there, you felt you could move mountains – and this wasn't all feminist groups, it was a cross-section, including the Mothers' Union. We were all united in what we were saying and feeling, until one point when we went to the city to 'lay claim to our cathedrals'.

We had prepared a wonderful liturgy: first we went to the Methodist Hall with a liturgy of words; then to the Anglican Cathedral with a liturgy of movement; and then to the Catholic Cathedral with a liturgy of music. The Methodist Hall was fine: the Free Churches knew how to handle feminism. They had been through all the ordination thing yonks ago, and were totally sensitive to us, and the Moderator, John Newton, gave us an entirely appropriate, one-sentence welcome.

But the moment we got to the Anglican Cathedral the trouble started, because they thought, 'This is a group come on pilgrimage, we will welcome them in the usual way.' And the usual way is that the bishop stands up and gives a talk about Liverpool's social deprivation. Now we had spent our whole weekend hearing voices from Liverpool about the social deprivation and didn't appreciate being preached at about it by a man.

And then it got worse. We went to the Catholic Cathedral where Archbishop Worlock greeted us with a speech about Our Lady, though there were hardly any Catholics there. And he and Bishop David Sheppard and the Methodist John Newton walked up and sat in three great thrones above us all. It didn't occur to them to do anything else. They were the three celebrants, as it were, the three presiding over the whole proceedings.

I was absolutely furious, and so were half the other women. But the other half of the women couldn't see anything wrong with it, and so it split the conference down the middle. A group of us – myself as a Catholic, and an Anglican woman, Judith Maltby, and a Free-Church woman who later became the moderator of the United Reformed Church general assembly, Ruth Clarke – wrote a joint letter to the two bishops, very politely explaining that they had put their foot in it, and thirty-five other women signed it. We thanked the bishops for their support but regretted that 'in the context of a conference which is concerned with empowering women to reclaim their full voice in our church, we were met by two substantial speeches by men'.

We got very stuffy answers. They simply couldn't see what the problem was. So there I found myself suddenly being one of 'those awful militant types'.

Then I got on to the ordination question, which I hadn't attended to at first, because of feeling that the primary struggle was for the laity. One summer holiday I read a book edited by Monica Furlong called *Feminine in the Church* (SPCK, 1984), and I just came straight out of that book and joined the Movement for the Ordination of Women. It is not that it changed my mind about anything, but it made me think about the issue enough to feel this is something terribly, terribly important.

ELAINE: That's fascinating. What strikes me in your story is how quickly being a self-conscious woman in the church took a shape and a form, whereas for me it was very different. I realized by now that I was a kind of feminist. I didn't really know what kind, but I cared passionately about women, particularly about oppressed women. I had heard some sobering stories in the classroom from ordinary women who had been dealt a very raw deal. For example, they had little education, which to me was very important. But also they often lacked resources as mothers. Many of them were poor, with unemployed husbands or no husbands at all, and on social security benefit. Later I met women who had gone through beatings and abuse, who were incest survivors, or living with persistent adulterers. After being at a distance from all this for so long, I felt the weight of how women struggle.

Tutoring with the Open University developed my feminism in a theoretical way, too, and I found that everything within me was beginning to weld together, as a Christian, a mother, a feminist, an academic and so on. But my feminism wasn't really addressed to the church at all. Feminists in the church seemed too caught up in a 'churchy' type agenda, whereas my feminism focused on women's everyday lives.

I would go to OU summer school and teach on the gender module of the social science foundation course. Every social science student would have to take this. In those days we taught it in women pairs: six of us team teaching. It felt like a kind of sisterhood every summer school, where we spent free time together, too. It was liberating and emancipating, and great fun. In Scotland, the six of us would go and walk on the hills, and talk and laugh. I also took part in the summer school for the women's studies programme where the programme was more radically feminist. There would be women-only discos, no men allowed, so all the usual disco agendas of finding a bed-partner for the night were written out. Women would throw their shoes off and dance together or in groups with sheer exhilaration. Older women, women in wheelchairs, would all let their hair down and have a fantastic evening. Those people who didn't normally enjoy much of a social life found themselves freed up. It was wonderful. The hilarious thing is that it was the one disco at summer school that every man wanted to get in on. They would be outside, literally lining up, pestering to be admitted. We would have the biggest butch women there as bouncers, throwing all these men off the premises!

The women's disco was one of the highlights of my week, because it was where women could enjoy themselves in an atmosphere of non-sexism, and do all kinds of idiotic things that women can do together. And it was a very liberating experience for many women. Of course, there were women who needed to have men at every disco for some reason,

and found the idea of women-only very off-putting. But
even they came along, and were nearly always won over.
I think hundreds of women found this new experience very
different.

So my years with the Open University were a wonderful
time for me. In addition to being a good place academically,
it helped to shape up my kind of feminism. For me it was
Christian, but non-clerical and non-ecclesiastical. It was to do
with transmitting the essence of the gospel to the normality
of women's lives.

I did invite women to come to church because I believed
they would hear the Christian gospel more fully there, and be
drawn to God. But when one woman took up the invitation,
the effect was not what I had, naively, expected. Her comment
afterwards was simply, 'Gosh!' and I suddenly saw the service
through her eyes. Men had taken charge of everything – the
sermon, the service, the prayers – and the hymns, language
and liturgy had all embodied exclusively male language. It
had been alienating for a woman. She looked at me with
bewilderment, and I could see she was thinking – 'How can a
feminist like you ...?'

I suppose it was about then that I realized that I was not
living an integrated life. I had accepted church as it was, and
not applied the same standards to it that I had applied everywhere else.

In the middle of all this we went to live in the United
States, where I taught women's studies in a sociology programme. In one college my students included the wives of
academic staff, and that caused a few ripples. They were from
the Christian Reformed Church background, where there was
then a notable gender divide. The women who came along to
my classes began to change their outlook and some of their
habits, and colleagues would phone me and ask, jokingly,

'What have you done to my wife?' But I still think it was jolly good for all of them. They were great people.

After we came back to England to live I wrote my first book, *What's Right with Feminism* (SPCK, 1985). The idea was to communicate something about the Christian gospel to secular feminists whom I wanted to put in touch with God. I've always wanted to help others to know the Creator of heaven and earth, and the truth about our own need for God's forgiveness. Yet as I researched and wrote, I began more and more to see that a big problem for a lot of these women is the church. Because even though patriarchy is woven into the whole of secular society, everyone acknowledges that. The church, however, pretends it's not there.

This was reinforced by my experience as a part-time lecturer at an Anglican theological college. I liked most of the students, had some great colleagues, but the whole atmosphere breathed a kind of sexism of the kind that I'd been unaware of earlier in my life. The layers of assumptions that had been internalized were so multi-layered that when you started to unpack one you realized that behind that was another, and another. It took ages to wade through the layers. I remember two incidents in particular. I was once passing through the reception lobby when an elderly visiting bishop appeared in the doorway. He saw me and obviously thought 'woman, therefore general servant'. So he headed confidently towards me and said indulgently, 'Be a good girl, will you, and make me a quick cup of tea, and let the principal know I'm here?' I was flabbergasted! I could only reply, 'Terribly sorry, I have to deliver a philosophy lecture right now, but there's a kettle in the student kitchen.' The other incident involved one of two difficult colleagues. For the third time running he hadn't shown up in chapel when I was on the preaching rota. I decided to tackle him. 'Do you think I preach heresy?' I asked.

'Is my teaching unorthodox?' 'Not at all,' he replied, 'and it's nothing personal. It's just that you're a woman.' I'm still wondering what could be more personal than that.

So writing a book and teaching at theological college turned me into the feminist I now am. It transmuted my optimism about what the church could do for women, into a much more sober feminism of recognizing that the church often presents one of the biggest obstacles to a woman's growth before God.

MARGARET: How did that develop?

ELAINE: It coincided with the start of our Men, Women and God movement which addressed the gender divisions from a Christian viewpoint. It was launched when my book was launched, and identified a lot of issues for women from an evangelical constituency that nobody had named before.

About five hundred women turned up for our first conference in 1985. We were amazed at it. Again they were from all kinds of backgrounds. I don't think the word 'feminism' had ever been articulated in an evangelical context – it was anathema, really. It was always something that other women and other groups did.

Evangelicals thought they didn't have the range of problems that feminist theology addressed. We didn't have a problem with the Virgin Mary, with the over-clericalism of the church or with the scriptures because we understood the scriptures, whereas other groups didn't. Now we were admitting that there were problems here, multi-layered ones which we wanted to address.

In 1985 there were two conferences. Our Men, Women and God conference in London, and another in Birmingham, a month later, which again attracted huge numbers. I spoke at both and was amazed that so many evangelical women were suddenly becoming involved with scripture, hermeneutics and gender issues. Many of them had been used to the kind of sermons which largely ignored the women's stories in the Gospels, or else interpreted them in a patronizing way. So even to recover these together helped us to see Christ in a new depth. It led us on to hermeneutical questions and to issues about ordination, and so much more.

The conferences continued. A later one in 1990 was very different. After a morning of workshops, the main focus was a dance presentation, based upon an extended poem by Stewart Henderson, and co-presented by Carol Henderson – both amazingly talented people. The themes of creation, Fall, redemption, which I had also taken in my book, formed the structure for the work, and Springs Dance Company performed the dance. Carol or Stewart read the poetry which shaped the dance movements, and then the dance took place to music and no words were spoken at all. The effect was quite extraordinary.

There was one particular sequence interpreting the story of the woman bent double. The dance conveyed the physical struggle of handicap and the emotional turmoil within. Then the woman meets the Christ who uncripples and liberates her, helping her to unfold slowly and be free from pain. There's a wonderful sequence where she begins to open up, as a full human being – a woman coming back to life – to reach out to the endless possibilities, and sharing her joy and delight with others around her. Her movements were fluid and perfect. Then, little by little, as she is exalting in her wonderful new-found freedom, the power of patriarchal control starts to close in on her, and eventually surround her. As she tries to find more freedom, and retain the freedom she has got, they press in on her, restraining every move, and she begins to bend over again, and is finally left twisted and bent double, back on the floor.

It was a powerful but frightening message, that the church can actually take away the liberation that Christ brings. People were moved, shaken, and many asked for prayer and counselling afterwards, because they felt they had taken part in that kind of oppression. At the end of the piece there was complete silence and then great applause. The fact that the message about Christ's liberation can be expressed in many different forms is so exciting. I think it points to the whole-ness and integration of our lives before God.

MARGARET: I think one of the more recent and exciting experiences for me was that Hothouse discussion on feminism at Greenbelt that we both took part in, largely because of the numbers at what was planned as a little, cosy event. They were absolutely packed in. To see that interest coming from Christians from such a wide variety of backgrounds, including so many evangelicals, is a reflection of something that is a reality in all the churches. There is massive interest.

At the first weekend conference I spoke at after *Motherhood and God* came out in 1984, they said just that: 'We had been trying to get weekends going on this and that topic, and we didn't get many coming. This one is suddenly booked up and now we know what to put on.'

ELAINE: Over the years I have become more sober in my expectations of the church. I don't over-expect now, and I am prepared to make a lot more allowances for people who are on different stages of the journey from me. I want to see some progress – whether from men or women – in moving into a more expansive and liberating grasp of the gospel. But never-theless, I want to nudge rather than batter them towards that.

Two

BEING A FEMINIST
MOTHER

♀ **ELAINE:** Should we talk about children and the way
we pass our ideas on to them? I have three boys,
whose growth has been contemporary with my feminism. The
first two were brought up pretty much equally by my husband
and myself so they didn't see fixed gender roles. Apart from
my role in breastfeeding, Alan would be as likely to be in a
nurturing role as I was. And we have both shared housework
and we tried to make sure at least one of us was always at
home when they were small. I think we felt, from the beginning on, because we thought as a family, travelled as a family
and were very integrated, that there weren't many problems.

Some problems did come when they went to school.
Inevitably, children are exposed to all kinds of ideas that are
not part of their parents' journey. Well-meaning teachers in
the classroom would reinforce sexist ideas at a very young age.
I remember being present when one teacher asked a classroom
of eleven-year-olds for 'two strapping boys to carry the desk'.
But in that class the only strapping eleven-year-olds were girls.

We've always been keen to communicate deep respect for
women and empathy with women's ideas, while trying to give
our sons freedom to reflect on their own masculinity. I don't
know whether we have succeeded or not.

Our two oldest sons have turned out to be scientists and mathematicians while our youngest is more involved with music and humanities. Our oldest, now married, shares the patterns of responsibility which most oldest siblings have, and we are grateful that he works hard at keeping in touch. He and his middle brother are 'ideas' persons, and both of them give us stimulating discussions. They are equally good cooks. Our youngest is an empathizer, who shares his feelings and has a well-developed language of emotions. We've learnt a great deal from all three of them and they've all been influenced by Christian feminism.

Those issues of masculinity and femininity that have been absorbed as part of my own progress and lifestyle, I have had to re-work and articulate in terms of bringing my children up. It's difficult to measure success. Have we managed to counter the big divides in our culture in a way that helps them towards lives that are more whole? I hope so.

MARGARET: I have three children: boy, girl, boy. Before we had children we had a theory that we wouldn't have sex roles. And to some extent, I think we achieved it in the beginning. I was a 'bad housewife', with absolutely no ambition in that direction, in fact despising the notion of being that sort of a woman.

After having three children it became more and more evident that the theory of no sex roles had failed. When you have children you have an enormous explosion of work. So there has been a massive compromise, which I have been prepared to make because other things are more important.

ELAINE: Yes, I would be prepared to go along with that compromise. Even now, I can come home and the washing up isn't done, and of course that's because none of us in the house deeply cares when the washing up is done. Most of the time I don't care any more than anyone else, but every now and then I do care, so I do it. Over all the years I would say Alan has done most of the washing up in the house, I do more of the general housework and two of our boys have both been very domesticated. But I am still more likely to be the one who reacts to a mess and gives up time to clear it up. And you're right, it's a compromise.

MARGARET: That is so common. A great friend of mine at Cambridge, a sympathetic man, has admitted this. He said, 'I try to do what I can in the house, and yet always it's my wife who is up later than I am, tidying up, doing the washing up. I think I have done my bit but she is always up doing something more.' It seems to be an almost universal experience of women that no matter what time you get back at night, the kitchen is there for you to clean up.

Now in terms of giving an example to children, I don't know. I really don't know. I mean certainly our children would be very opposed to sexism, just as they feel very strongly about racism and classism. It would be interesting to see, as they get older, whether in fact sexism is breaking through again, and I suspect to some extent it will do so.

But I do feel there is a genuine problem for women that is probably insoluble. You can have the theory of sharing everything and yet – though in your case it doesn't seem so evident – the whole childbearing thing does seem to take women out, and take them out by their own choice. They are tired when they are pregnant; they are breastfeeding; and there is also the homeliness bit, which I have come to recognize in myself. Not that I am a good housewife, but there is a sort of burgeoning housewife in me that would like – when I have the time and so on, which isn't often – to make a lovely home.

And there clearly are psychological differences between the sexes, though one dare not pin them down. The juggling between family and work for women seems to be a real result of the Fall. Every woman seems to struggle with it, and there isn't an answer, except to do what one can. The business of having children in itself is difficult, because if you have them too young then you haven't had your education, and if you have them too old then you get tired, and so on. There doesn't seem to be the right age to do any of these things, or the right choices.

I mean, we all care very much that there aren't more women in Parliament, and yet what woman would actually choose to have an MP's life, apart from a single woman, or one who has had twins and got it all over quickly? It is a difficult choice for a woman to make, and I am not even sure that she should make it until the children have grown up and gone away, because of the hours.

ELAINE: But in a funny sense – and I don't think it's nostalgia, or romantically re-writing history – I still feel that the most fulfilling time of my life was when my children were small and I was at home. I don't believe this is because there is something inherent in a woman that makes her more domestically suited. It's more to do with not having other pressures or things to think about.

Some think this is out of kilter with feminism, but I really did enjoy having small, growing, intelligent little beings around me to cluck over. I remember the animation in their faces as they shared with me something exciting that they had just made or discovered. I think it was something to do with having the freedom and the time to tap into tiny, growing humans who hadn't been contaminated with all the sorrows of adulthood, and hadn't had to wade through the cares of the world. It was being surrounded with young life which I found very enriching, very exciting, very lovely. And looking back I still find that period wonderful and would not have had it any other way.

I loved teaching my children when they were young. I loved exploring places with them, making up stories, taking them to grandparents, playing football. I remember when our youngest was about seven he brought me along to the park for a game with the other kids, and they stared at me with horror and protested, 'You haven't brought your mum?!'

To some extent being with children is like being given permission to return to a kind of childhood yourself, and put on hold unpleasant things about life, or deal with them at a very familial or concrete level. I was so aware that I could make a big difference to my own children. I couldn't make much difference right then to all those women out there who are aching and struggling under the oppression of all kinds of systems, but here at home I could do something that nobody else could. Of course, I knew that sooner or later I would have to go and do something about the bigger picture, but right then, I had other priorities. And I found being around with these lovely boys sheer enjoyment.

MARGARET: That's interesting, because that bit is very, very different for me. I found having small children at home very difficult – my most frustrating time and my greatest experience of imprisonment, really – because of them being so demanding. If I could do it for two hours, that would be OK. But it was all day long. You couldn't go to the bathroom without them causing some accident somewhere, you couldn't read a book because they wouldn't let you, you couldn't go to a lecture because you would have to organize a babysitter, and so on. I found that very difficult. Hearing you talk about it,

I feel, 'Gosh, how wonderful, I wish I had felt like that.' But actually I didn't.

What I did absolutely adore was being pregnant, and having a tiny baby as long as it was still at the silent stage, before it was mobile. I loved being pregnant, maybe partly because it took me a few months to get pregnant – it wasn't very long actually, but it felt like ages at the time and I realized how desperately I did want children. I still feel very warm thinking back on that sense of life within me, that intimacy – a sort of image of being held within God or of holding God within us – that tremendous closeness and warmth and love, the perfection of the harmony of it, and the hiddenness of the mystery of it.

And then holding a little child, the fragility, the preciousness of it. I still feel that way. But it is a different matter when they get a bit older.

ELAINE: Yes, they are demanding, and I think it would have been different for me had we not both been parenting at a fairly equal level for most of that time. There were so many built-in times when I wasn't in charge of the children, and could go to college to teach for an hour or a day, and so on. These times were completely different from being at home with the children.

Alan made a huge priority of being at home whenever his timetable allowed. As a college lecturer he had some flexibility. He always used to get up early in the morning, get the children to school, and leave himself. I would dozily follow him up. But then he could be home straight after lunch, and sometimes work in the evenings, or on Saturdays.

But there was enough variation in the day to mean he was home for many daylight hours during the week. What for other people would have been unsociable hours were for us enormously sociable hours, because those were times when the boys were awake and around. And as they grew older, we did the timetabling differently, but it always gave me enough times to break from the routine.

And we travelled a lot as a family. As soon as college had finished, we would bung everything in the car, tent and the lot, and just drive away. We didn't know where we were going to, and sometimes we didn't come back for five or six weeks. That time together was bliss. We would spend some marvellous holidays in Cornwall and Devon, or abroad on the Continent. We had no cares, few responsibilities and, again, flexible roles. The only fixed ritual was that Alan and the boys put the tent up while I cooked the meal. It was a tremendous period for me because it gave me time and capacity really to enjoy the stages of motherhood rather than making them a huge chore. And I am profoundly grateful.

MARGARET: Now, about bringing up children and introducing them to God in a non-sexist way: I tried to bring them up from the very beginning familiar with the idea that there was no sex in God, but without thumping it too hard, you know. I am aware that sometimes it's both necessary and good to thump the she-ness of God. But with your children, particularly if they are boys, I do feel it's important they don't get more than 50 per cent female pronouns, and actually less than that, because they also have to learn to tune into the church's language and expressions. If they are brought up with something too unfamiliar the juxtaposition is too difficult. But they grew up very happily and easily with the idea that God is both father and mother, both he and she. Just as God is all kinds of combinations of extraordinary opposites.

ELAINE: That's fascinating. I am still growing in my understanding of God. What was never important, theologically, early on in my Christian growth, means more now. And my perception of God is always getting bigger and deeper. When the children were very small, much of it was still foreign territory for me. But as they grew up I was able to share my own growth in this area with them, and they have listened and taken on board a lot of what I've shared, which has been encouraging. What we have encouraged them to do is always to stay open in mind in their attitude towards God and each other, and not dismiss some other Christian's experience or understanding of God just because it has not been theirs. That is sometimes a battle in the evangelical community.

My own upbringing was Anglo-Catholic, I didn't become an evangelical until much later.

MARGARET: Your upbringing was Anglo-Catholic?

ELAINE: Yes. My mother's church in Horbury was strongly Anglo-Catholic and I was raised in that tradition. There was a convent round the corner, and nuns whom I always felt were locked away behind barbed wire. The walls were high, with broken pieces of glass on top, and the chapel had a musty smell. Going back to something like that now would be very strange, because it is so different from the way I worship these days.

MARGARET: So what brought you into the evangelical wing?

ELAINE: I think it was because I hadn't got a deep sense of God from the Anglo-Catholic tradition. The local parish church which we actually attended was not so high as Horbury, but of the same ilk. Much was to do with ritual, learning catechisms, learning responses, knowing the right things to do at the right times. I accepted all that. I suppose the focus of our church was to teach you these things in the hope that, when you learned the meaning of them all, your relationship with God would just flow naturally.

The old bachelor vicar was a kindly and pastoral man, but there wasn't much emphasis on prayer, and none at all on personal Bible study. The Bible was a great mystery to me – we just had readings from the lectionary, with no obvious beginning or end and no explanation. As a younger girl, our next-door neighbour had taken me to the Congregational Sunday School, which was more informal (but, I felt, not very 'holy'). But it was really the Methodists, who lugged me along to a youth camp in my mid-teens, who presented me with the gospel so loved by evangelicals – that we were sinners and Christ died for our sins. My reaction was, 'What?! What is this about?'

Yes, there was a need in my life for a deeper and more clear, more coherent relationship with God, and I responded to that. I had to unlearn a lot of the rather glib optimism I'd accepted, when I went to university, and recognize the Christian faith is also about struggle. But I've stayed within an evangelical focus, I feel comfortable and at home there.

MARGARET: At least two of our children now are totally out of any church belief or practice, and I am aware that the sexism of the church is one very large factor in that. It just makes the whole business incredible and absurd, and something that they don't even desire to be part of.

ELAINE: I think that is very painful, appalling. It must be as painful for men as for women who have been brought up in this way. When sometimes one of my sons has commented about some sexism and asked how women cope with it, I say, 'It's not just our problem, it's yours as well.'

The question for the next generation is whether they will carry on identifying with the church, in spite of its pessimism, its boredom, sexism, irrelevance and all the other things. I want them desperately to continue, because I think that they must reform the church from within rather than become apathetic or disillusioned and just bolt. Otherwise, the church stays simply as it is. I want my children's generation in the church to bring about the miracle. And so far, I like what I see. Under God, it is possible. And I'm now at the stage where I learn from them.

Three

GOD, LANGUAGE AND THE TRINITY

♀ **MARGARET:** Is God male, female or neuter? And the Trinity? How do we use inclusive language for God?

ELAINE: There are two issues, aren't there? Who God is, and how we speak about God. At what stage does language about God begin to be important to us? Because at the beginning it really wasn't important for me. God was God, and I never stopped much to think about God's gender, or even language about God. There wasn't an issue. I took for granted the metaphors and similes that I carried around about God. Occasionally I thought them a bit lopsided, sometimes militaristic. But I accepted that they were simply 'givens'. It was really relatively recently that language became an issue at all.

Is the same true for you or have these issues always been there for you?

MARGARET: I think that must have been true for me as well. It started to matter for me when I wrote *Motherhood and God* (Geoffrey Chapman, 1984). My point of view up till then had been, 'Of course everybody knows that God isn't male, but there is no problem about it. It's a convention, it's acceptable.'

In the process of writing *Motherhood and God* I began immediately to see it as rather more important than that, and really to see the whole of feminist theology resting most fundamentally on how we understand God. Because if that complementarity is there in the Godhead, then that is what we are drawing on when we work out feminism through the church.

At the time I wrote that book, 1984, it was still very odd to call God 'she' or to use the metaphor of mother. But it wasn't yet a disputed issue because no one was doing it. It was only when people began to do it that others started reacting. Then it became important to assert the validity of it.

ELAINE: In the Anglican church, and Protestant churches as a whole, to call God 'mother' was to nail your colours to the mast. It was doing more than trying to find an inclusive way of addressing God. It was also quite a strong political statement. When the Church of Scotland did something on the motherhood of God it virtually broke the whole women's movement in the Church of Scotland asunder.

MARGARET: That was in 1982, and the report came out at just the same time as my book.

ELAINE: I was there some years after and still in the aftermath, when a lot of people were arguing that these radical feminists had attempted a takeover of the General Assembly and had forced a political agenda. And those involved would no doubt admit that they were trying to do something definite to raise people's attention to the issue.

So that was always the problem. Attempts to restrict patriarchal influences and get away from a gendered God were always seen as buying into a political agenda.

MARGARET: At the time when I wrote *Motherhood and God* we were beginning to have Christian feminism, and it was generally not much liked. It was found divisive. Now it has permeated throughout the church and is expressed at all sorts of levels. But then it felt more a matter of people complaining, people knocking down the past, and I could understand the resistance.

And I felt it was very, very important that if one called God 'mother', it should not be a ploy – in order to achieve the end of women's ordination or some other political end in the church. The most fundamental reason had to be to understand God better, and to speak a language that was more adequate to the infinity of God. That is something I still feel very strongly.

ELAINE: That has been exactly my motivation too. What follows from it – the impact on women's lives, the affirmation of women as human beings made in the image of God and so on – is secondary to the bigger issue which lies at the heart: who is God?

Our language so easily shrinks God. For language is a human construct, and we are trying to talk about divine realities. It is difficult not to talk about God in ways that are limiting and constricting. The more we can be linguistically flexible, drawing on the breadth of biblical images, feminine and masculine, and recognize that our language can only represent and not embody God, the better. The end has to be, as you say, to understand God better, draw closer to God, and make God more widely accessible to other people. It has to be to proclaim the gospel to the full, to tell the good news to women, to speak the truth about God.

I always worried when people protested 'Of course we don't believe in a male God,' but then almost in the next breath signified that, even if not male, this God was still patriarchal. What was the point of having a neutered, patriarchal God? You might as well have a male, patriarchal God. In relinquishing a God who is male, we need to be more careful about ways we speak.

MARGARET: The very fact that when we began to do it people found it difficult, was an indication that it was needed. Once people began to say, 'I don't like to think of God as a mother,' or 'God as "she" sounds like a foreign God, not the Christian God,' then one became aware that their God was too small. So the fact of it feeling odd was an indication of how much it was needed.

ELAINE: Yes. The success of an ideology is the way in which it becomes normal in our lives and defines our parameters and our perspective. The fact that some people in the church find it hard to talk of God as a mother, even though there is biblical precedence for it in Job 38 or Isaiah 30, indicates to me the enormous success of the ideology. Our minds become crippled and not even open to the breadth of biblical imagination and disclosure. We end up going down tramlines, rather than being able to walk freely before the God who is bigger by far than our language.

MARGARET: Perhaps I could bring in a Catholic point. The mother imagery for Catholics has traditionally been attached to the character called Our Lady (whom I now prefer to call Mary of Nazareth). Mary, the mother of Jesus, had syphoned off all that mother talk. Up to a point I think that is perfectly legitimate and can be very helpful, but beyond a certain point it takes something away from the Godhead.

When you get to the point where people are saying, 'I'll pray to Our Lady because she will understand better, she's the really compassionate one,' then you are beginning to bring forward a false image of God.

I don't know which is worse really, because, on the other hand, the objection brought against the Protestant side, where there was no Our Lady figure, was that there isn't any female element there at all.

My position is that it is quite legitimate to have an idea of Mary as our mother, as long as we understand that the fundamental mother and the root of all motherhood is God. There is a wonderful quote from Julian of Norwich: 'That fair lovely word "mother" is so sweet and so kind in itself that it cannot truly be said of anyone or to anyone except of him and to him who is the true Mother of life and of all things' (*Showings*, chapter 60).

The Church of Scotland report, *The Motherhood of God* (St Andrew Press, 1984), which was the fruit of the dispute that you mentioned, was a very good report, and it had a very clear passage about religious analogy. The conservative woman on that report took basically the same line as William Oddie took in his book *What Will Happen to God?*, which also came out the same year (SPCK, 1984).

They were saying that you could, if you really insisted, say God was like a mother, but once you start leaving out the 'like' you get into trouble, because you move from what is clearly a simile to a religious analogy.

A true religious analogy, they said, was something that was done with 'father', but you are not at liberty to do it with 'mother'. So the objection was that there is a distinction between a simile – which is just, 'In some ways God is like ...' – and a religious analogy – which is something much more profound and says, 'In the deepest sense, all fatherhood that is on heaven and earth gets its name from God.'

Now I want to maintain that it is quite valid to do that with 'mother' as well, and I think that quote from Julian of Norwich gives some support from the tradition. That is to say, when we become mothers we are drawing on a maternal love which has its root and origin in God. That is what is feeding our mother-love, even if we don't know God. God is where this extraordinary quality of mother-love comes from. God is more truly a mother than we are.

ELAINE: That is an incredibly powerful argument and when I first encountered that in your own writing the simplicity of it took my breath away. There is an unanswerable quality to the argument. Because someone who wants to say, 'But no, you are actually overdoing or abusing the simile,' or 'You are now moving into analogy,' has got another question to answer. And that is, 'What is the source of all motherhood?'

And I think that is a question that I have not heard answered by these people. They usually fall back on the old dualistic dichotomy which is there in a lot of patristic writings, that somehow fatherhood – identified as rationality, discipline, care, protectiveness and so on – comes from God, but motherhood comes from our humanness, our animal nature, our links with the earth and so on. And that fuels another kind of feminist reaction, which is to say, 'OK, let's be like that then, let's celebrate the earth and earthiness and all the rest of it.'

But the other route is to say, 'No, there is no dualism there. Both of these find their fullness in God, and what we are experiencing as mothers is something very close to the heart of God, and the heart of God is the love, the compassion, the self-giving and sacrificial vulnerability that we know as mothers.' For me this is a wonderful argument and I am enormously indebted to you for it.

I don't think the critics have any cogent response, especially in light of what they then want to say about the Christian faith and the scriptures. It can leave a big hole in the middle of their theologies. Who are we? Who are mothers? What are they doing?

The worst possible set of responses is, of course, where fatherhood comes from God and motherhood is there as a response to fatherhood and in obedience to it. In other words, motherhood is derivative: mothers are there to obey fathers who are the ones who give the structure and interpret God's rules for living. Once you have moved into that (and I know a lot of people who do argue that way, if pushed very hard!) we are left with a troublesome justification for the patriarchal way in which society has been structured and of the terrible things some ('disobedient') women have suffered. But it seems a long way from a biblical ontology.

MARGARET: Biology is quite important here, in that at the stage when people thought that a girl-child was a sort of incomplete boy-child, then it made perfectly good logical sense to say that the perfect human form is the male form. That the male is more in the image of God than the female. Therefore you complimented God by talking about him as 'father', and we would denigrate God by reducing her to 'mother'.

When the female ovum was not yet discovered, and people thought of the creative power being just in the male seed, while the female only offered a nurturing environment which allowed it to grow, then the notion of God as creator had to be related to God as 'father'. The 'mother' was the nurturing environment which corresponded more naturally to the church. The biology has changed and theology needs to catch up with it.

Shall we come to the Trinity now?

ELAINE: Yes, let's do that.

MARGARET: This is one of the most difficult areas for feminism, I think. The idea is extraordinarily widespread that at least two of the three persons, 'Father, Son and Holy Spirit', are male. Now I would want to dispute that, and say that it is metaphorical language that we use for the trinitarian relationship, nothing actually to do with male or female.

Of course, if you start renaming the persons of the Trinity Life-giver, Pain-bearer, Love-maker, for example, as Jim Cotter does, people get very cross. They want to say 'Father, Son and Holy Spirit' is fundamental and any renaming is a distortion.

Then there is a fundamental divide in trinitarian theology, between those who see the Trinity as defined by their mutual inter-relationship – what is called the immanent Trinity – and those who see it defined by the way it affects the world – what is called the economic Trinity.

Yet most people do think along those lines: they see the Father as the one who created everything in the beginning, the Son as the one who came to redeem us, and the Spirit as the one who is left behind after the Son went away.

I think strict dogmatists say that is a crudification and strictly speaking the persons are differentiated only by means of their mutual relationships. But whichever way one thinks of it, one can put up a case for there not being a maleness in it.

Take the Father. That's the most difficult in a way, yet what I would argue is that the relationship of Father to Son is a metaphor from human reproduction, and what's actually behind it is the notion of generation, eternal generation of the second person out of the first person.

There is a wonderful quote from the Eleventh Council of Toledo in 675, one of the most important councils for trinitarian doctrine, which says that the Son 'is begotten or born not from nothing or from any other substance, but from the womb of the Father'. That's a wonderful mixed metaphor, and I see it as giving some legitimacy from tradition to the idea that maleness as such isn't part of the eternal trinitarian relationship. You can say, 'He is begotten,' but you can also say, 'He is born from the womb.'

The Son, of course, in the human incarnation, becomes a male human being. But the eternal second person of the Trinity was not male. He becomes male in the human incarnation. Now I don't know if you agree with that?

ELAINE: Yes, I do. But I want to go back to an earlier point you made. One of the earliest feminist ways of resolving the so-called maleness of the Trinity was to see the Holy Spirit as neuter or feminine, balancing out the Father and Son, but that left an equation of two to one, which resolved nothing. It wasn't helped either by throwing in Mary as an extra feminine voice!

MARGARET: As Jung did in his disastrous interpretation of the assumption as bringing a female fourth into a male trinity. It sold the whole pass.

ELAINE: So to your other points. There increasingly seems to be less difficulty with God the Father, for the reasons we've already mentioned: namely, the idea that 'Father' here incorporates father and mother, where the motherhood of God is a key expression of the nurturing heart of the Godhead. But coming to terms with the gender of God the Son is more problematic. Because evangelicals, I think rightly, make so much of God the Son, the Incarnate Word, much of our theology centres around the person and historicity of Christ. The problem is that people say, 'Ah, but when God was incarnate God came

as a male, and doesn't that tell us something about the nature
of God and the nature of man?' And the answer is, 'No'.

Most evangelical theologians have not been much enam-
oured of the idea of the functional Trinity – that is, that
the jobs are divided up and apportioned variously to God the
Father, Son and Spirit. There is a much bigger sense that the
Trinity is together at work in creation, in salvation, in the giving of wisdom. In the very beginning the Spirit is there,
brooding on the face of the waters (Genesis 1:2) and there are
many references to the Holy Spirit in the Hebrew scriptures.
And when the old patriarchs wrestled with God, or where in
the Old Testament there is a sense of God being physically
present, it is possible to think of that as the person of Christ,
the human form of God. This has been one of the evangelical
ways of responding. So the Trinity is at work throughout the
scriptures in creation and redemption.

Recently, however, I have entered into a deeper apprecia-
tion of the Trinity. For example, if we are made in the image of
God, then the fact that God is Trinity says something about
our humanness. I've found that extraordinarily liberating.
God as Trinity is a deeply relational God rather than God as a
self-subsisting, self-sufficient individual.

When an evangelical, brought up on the idea of the
authority of God the Father, is brought more deeply into contact with the relationality of God the Trinity it is emancipating and exciting.

Also it informs your spirituality at a much deeper level.
You move away from all the things that people have traditionally associated with maleness – isolation, individualism, being
able to sort things out on your own, not needing other
people, and so on: in other words, all the things that in our culture western men have been asked to emulate and live by. And
you move on to a much more feminine mode – communality,

commitment to community, networking, negotiation, needing one another, co-operation, being empathetic and so on.

So this communal model of God as Trinity has been so enriching to me over the last few years, and I have found it more and more exciting. It's also affirming, because if this is the God in whose image we are made, then that opens up the way for us to be more involved. Women have been trying to say for a very long time: we do want to be able to work in a more co-operative way, to be heard more, to hear one another and work things out together, we are not just here to obey some chap who is in authority.

And men too need this. Men too need relationality at the very depth of their being, to be able to develop and open it up in a fuller way. So I think trinitarian theology is a very enlivening and enriching development. There are women who have got there long before me, but it is nice to be there.

MARGARET: One of the things I find difficult about the Trinity is that our human model of relationship, the classic one, is man, woman, child. But that doesn't quite fit with the Trinity, does it?

ELAINE: No. There is equality, not hierarchy. There is mutual respect in every member of the Trinity.

I remember the passages in John, where Jesus twice has to explain to his disciples a little bit of what the Trinity is about, or tries to explain a little bit more about the Godhead to the people, in order that they too might be one.

So he draws on the very unity of the Godhead: 'The Father and I are one' (John 10:30) and 'The Holy Spirit, whom the Father will send in my name, will remind you of all that I have said' (John 14:26). There is a sense of unity, of indwelling in one another, in a beautifully mind-defying way. Then he asks us to do the same. To dwell within each other, and within God too. The Spirit lives within us, empowering us and working through us. It is a terrific model. And Christ's own words here are very helpful for me.

So we have this picture of the Trinity inviting us into relationship, both with the Godhead but also with each other. Being actively in relationship is the right way to be.

All these things are very encouraging. They also depart from what I was brought up on as a philosophy student, when I was confronted very thoroughly with the Enlightenment ideal of humanness, to be an individual, individuated, self-subsistent, rational substance.

This just blows away all of that. Even the idea that my humanness resides in my uniqueness is only half the story. The other part is that at the core of my uniqueness is my dependent relationship with God.

MARGARET: I just want to say one thing about the Spirit which might go aptly with what you were saying. I love it when Jerome points out that the Spirit is feminine in Hebrew, masculine in Latin, and neuter in Greek, 'for there is no sex in the divinity'. Although it can be useful to talk about the Spirit in female terms, it is not the answer. The femaleness is not just in the Spirit. It has to be in all three persons.

I still have a certain problem about all this, which is that although logically and doctrinally it is clear that there is no maleness, people keep on coming back and saying: 'Yes, but Jesus calls God "Father" over and over again. That is the privileged term.'

In the Old Testament 'Father' is not used much of God: someone added up the instances and found there were only eleven, and none of them a way of addressing God in prayer.

But obviously the Abba term, 'Father', was particularly precious, and was given to us to use as well as Jesus.

I always make it clear that I have got no hostility to 'Father'. And yet one wants to supplement it. An idea I have tried out, and often got quite a hostile reaction to, is that for Jesus the idea of having God as his father was terribly precious, because of not having a human father.

ELAINE: I think the 'Abba, Father' has also meant something else, in that Jesus is conveying to us that we too can have the relationship of a child to a parent with the almighty God of creation. It brings God's distance and otherness into our orbit. So we can ask something of this God – attention, concern, motherly compassion, protectiveness, care, nurture and so on. For me, calling God 'Abba' has always been permissive rather than limiting. We don't have to approach God only with awe and terror. We can call God 'Daddy' (or 'Mummy').

MARGARET: I think what you have said is absolutely crucial. Jesus calls God 'Abba' to make a point about God's intimacy to us. And people are now saying, 'Oh no, Father, but not Mother,' in order to do the opposite, to keep God at arm's length, and to say God is not mother.

Well, Jesus' whole point was to say, 'God is as close to us as the most loving and intimate parent.' He was not making a point about male and female, he was making a point about intimacy.

ELAINE: I agree entirely. And sometimes, in the Old Testament, where God is alluded to as father it is balanced by mother. The book of Job, for me, is a winner. The language is beautiful. There is that lovely passage where he asks Job...

MARGARET: 'From whose womb did the ice come forth, and who has given birth to the hoarfrost of heaven?' (Job 38:29).

ELAINE: Yes, with the implicit answer that the births came from the womb of God. And that's just after he has asked rhetorically, 'Has the rain a father, or who has begotten the drops of dew?' (Job 38:28). With the answer again: 'Yes, and I am that Father.' So there is the fatherhood and motherhood of God in very close proximity there.

MARGARET: The Old Testament doesn't often do that, but it does it enough, doesn't it? One can pull together half a dozen or so instances to show that the idea is there of God's motherhood.

There is the passage from Deuteronomy, for example, 'As an eagle stirs up its nest, and hovers over its young ... the Lord alone guided him' (Deuteronomy 32:11–12). And Psalm 131: 'I have calmed and quieted my soul, like a weaned child with its mother.' And the famous passage from Isaiah (though the theme recurs several times there in places which are less well known): 'Can a woman forget her nursing child, or show no compassion for the child of her womb? Even these may forget, yet I will not forget you' (Isaiah 49:15).

Yet is there still a question over why fatherhood, specifically fatherhood, was so much what Jesus taught? Does that create problems for us? It certainly creates problems for us in that people think it does.

ELAINE: It creates problems because we always want to take terms out of their cultural context and make them ontological. 'Father', in the culture in which Jesus was teaching his disciples, had enormous weight and strength. Acceptance by the father was the means to everything: to inheritance, to the future, to life, to well-being, to family relationships, love, to closeness, intimacy, to all that we could have. And the glorious thing is that Jesus is inviting us into that. God can be like this to us. We can have all of this in our relationship with God.

It is being in relationship with the Father that gives us everything. So, culturally, 'mother' could offer little of this. But we have to be careful when we translate what this means into our time. If we fix on the wrong understanding of 'father' – as an remote authoritarian, rather than the one who gives us access – we make God simply into some forbidding deity who is exacting and disciplining.

MARGARET: Jesus was making an inclusive point. An embracing and inclusive and welcoming point, and it has been turned into an exclusive, limiting point.

This reminds me of that new inclusive-language Bible, do you know about that? I had to answer a question about that on Nick Stuart's programme, *Many Questions*.

ELAINE: The new politically correct Bible?

MARGARET: Yes. I suggested that they talk about that and Nick Stuart said, 'I thought of that but I quickly discarded it because I thought I will never get anyone to say a word in favour of this Bible.'

I said, 'Oh, I will, I think it's a very good thing.' So we did it and it was quite a lively discussion.

They use 'father-mother' as a hyphenated term for God. Now I want to say that there is a legitimacy in that. Obviously in a way it is taking a liberty with the text, but – at least this is what I argued on the programme, let's see if you think it stands up – there are at least two ways in which fatherhood in

New Testament times meant something different from what it means today.

One is what I have already mentioned about the female ovum: that all the creativity, generative power, was seen in the male. Now that we understand you have sperm and egg, to say 'father-mother' is to capture the creativity more fully, and to that extent is a more adequate translation.

The other is that in that society inheritance was a male thing, father to son, father to son. So the Son does the Father's work (John 10:37), and we become adopted sons of the Father (Galatians 4:5). That meant something to people, but to be adopted daughters of God wouldn't mean the same.

ELAINE: And it was enormously liberating for women to see themselves as adopted sons, because it meant they had the same inheritance as a son. It had the reverse effect from what it has today. For women to be fully accepted into sonship, into inheritance, meant that they could have all that God has in store. But to be simply daughters would have left them outside all that.

Four

A MALE SAVIOUR

ELAINE: Perhaps we can talk this week about the second person of the Trinity. Is that all right with you?

MARGARET: Right. Personally this is what I find most difficult about being a Christian feminist. But curiously I don't find it difficult psychologically or spiritually, I only find it difficult theologically and theoretically.

ELAINE: That's an interesting division – most people find it the other way round. Theologically they are prepared to accept that God became incarnate in male form, but psychologically they can't relate to a male Christ, because they need someone who will understand what it is like to be a woman. So how is it the other way round for you?

MARGARET: I wonder whether I am actually enabled to relate to Jesus because I am a woman and he is a man. Because as a woman I like men. Now the relationship of a man to Jesus must be different in some way from my relationship to Jesus, because between people of different sexes there is an extra dimension to the relationship – complementarity, and searching for the other, and wonder at the differentness. So when I say I don't find it difficult psychologically and spiritually, I suspect that part of the answer is that as a woman I actually like having a male saviour to relate to. It makes me like to go and throw myself into his arms. Whereas with women, much as I love them, I don't want to do that.

Of course, women vary, because some have been damaged, whether by parental figures or by boyfriend or husband figures, in such a way that they feel safer with other women. That is quite a common feeling nowadays. But I don't quite feel that way. I go on liking men.

ELAINE: Let's stay with the experiential at the moment. If you look at the women who are recorded in the scripture as surrounding Christ, they seemed to have the same experience that you are describing. There is a ring of truth about it. They were women in a patriarchal society who nevertheless found in this man someone who didn't stand for all the stuff usually doled out to women. Clearly he must have been engaging and attractive to have women who wanted to be with him. He had a particularly close relationship with some: Mary and Martha, for example. Martha felt bold enough to tell him off when it seemed he had let them down over Lazarus.

MARGARET: Notably in that particular household, it is the two sisters that he relates to, and Lazarus is a shadowy figure.

ELAINE: Yes, you're right! Lazarus only crops up in the account when he dies.

MARGARET: 'See how he loved him,' it says, but all the evidence of the closeness is with the two women. I always feel that is Jesus' family, down in Judaea. That was his home, that was where he would flop for the nights when he wanted to get away from it all.

ELAINE: What's going on there is a level of intimacy and friendship – an affinity – which must have meant that these women too liked having Jesus around. They didn't find his gender in any sense a barrier. If anything, it probably felt warm, protective and affirming.

And look at the way he treated other women. The woman with menstrual problems is my favourite (Luke 8). And then the other women, the women disciples recorded in Luke 8. The wife of Herod's household manager, Joanna, what was she doing there? Why wasn't she at home with her husband? Or was he travelling as well? There is no indication that Jesus told her to pack off back home and make sure the household was being cared for.

Some of them travel a long way to be with Jesus, and the trek from Galilee to Jerusalem is an enormous one. So what was going on? We don't know. Their stories are not written down for us in the text, but there is clearly something magnetic about Jesus.

MARGARET: Think of the number of Christians who go on about Christianity as the family religion, yet it always seems to me that no one attacked the family in the way Jesus did. I preached a sermon in an Oxford college, where the congregation was extremely Christian Union, on the theme of Jesus as the one who challenged the family and invited people to leave their family. And they loved it, because all the way through I was quoting the Bible. That is what evangelicals like, so they didn't notice what an unorthodox message was coming out. The method was right.

ELAINE: I think what was going on in those passages is that the identity that women had always traditionally had in the family wasn't enough. Their identity had to be somewhere else, in their own relationship to God. That is what Jesus gave them. It took priority over all the other relationships.

MARGARET: I am thinking of two other women: the woman at the well – that was one of my chapters in *Six New Gospels* (Geoffrey Chapman, 1994), and I imagined the sexual vibes of that encounter – and Mary Magdalene in the garden – her being flooded with tears, and him coming up with a word, and her turning, and him saying, 'Don't cling to me.' There is a tremendous man–woman dynamism there.

ELAINE: I think that is certainly there in the gospels. It is evident with the woman at the well, to the extent that even the disciples don't seem sure about what Jesus is doing talking to a woman, particularly this sort of woman. We know about her sexual history because Jesus tells us. But we also recognize that she has a history of vulnerability as well. She has been divorced by a lot of husbands. She is very much an abandoned woman, who is now living with someone who can't be bothered to do the right thing by her in that society.

Another woman, of course, is the woman who anoints him. That is an incredibly sensual encounter – the touching of the flesh, the caressing of the feet. There is physical contact which in the context of orthodox Judaism is striking. Most rabbis would run a mile.

MARGARET: But does this create a problem in the other direction? We started off from the question: 'Is it difficult for women to relate to Jesus because he is a man?' But what about the question: 'Is it difficult for men to relate to Jesus because he is a man?' If women have this special way of relating to him, then what are men missing out on? They can't really be missing out on something important, can they?

ELAINE: I don't know the answer to that, not being a man! But it is interesting that certain men relate better to Jesus than other men, and I think they are the men who have engaged more with their own sexuality and their emotional lives. I have talked to a lot of men who said what they like about Jesus is his power and his authority and his goodness, but there is not that same emotional connection.

A lot of men are drawn to Jesus because of the concept of sacrifice that we are going to look at next time. That is not a big thing for me: I am profoundly grateful that Christ died, I am full of admiration and so on, but that is not my point of engagement. It is more on this level of sheer intimacy and love.

MARGARET: It reminds me of one man who did the Spiritual Exercises with me, and I gave him to imagine having his feet washed by Christ at the Last Supper. He came back after doing this and said: 'Oh, it was boring. I sat there and I thought, "Here is Jesus washing my feet," and I tried to stay with it but it was boring.'

ELAINE: I wouldn't have found that at all boring! Another thing about Jesus in a relationship with women is that a lot of the women he encountered seemed to be in tears. That struck me recently. The menstruating woman is in tears because she has spent all that money, and she is terrified of what is going to happen because she has touched this religious teacher. The woman who anoints him is in tears because she seems over-come with love and gratitude. Martha and Mary are in tears over the death of Lazarus.

The sense of being overwhelmed by personal defeat and fear and all the emotions which are there in women's lives, but also by Christ's own kindness. He never demeans or dismisses women's tears, or objects that they are irrational, emotional people. He always seems to deal with them gently and with respect. And Jesus has his own tears when Lazarus dies. That connects him with the weeping women in another kind of way.

MARGARET: And then there is Mary Magdalene in the garden. Something that is interesting there is that some feminists, as Elisabeth Moltmann-Wendel points out, don't like the ones who cry. They like Martha, you know, because she is more sensible. But Mary of Bethany and her tears, they think is soppy and a stereotype. Maybe I am a weepy woman, but I like the tears.

But again – I don't know the answer to this, it is a genuinely interesting question – do women and men have the same sort of relationship with Jesus? I would want to assert that they have an equal relationship, but is it equal in the same way or is it equal in a different way?

ELAINE: I don't know how I would find out. I don't know, for example, how Alan's relationship with Jesus is different from mine.

MARGARET: When I pray I don't feel that Jesus being a man is a barrier. And yet at the same time I am asking myself, 'Why isn't it a barrier? Ought it to be a barrier?' But the fact is that I don't feel it as one.

ELAINE: Yes, I have never ever felt Christ's maleness as any kind of barrier. But then I wonder if that is because I was brought up as a traditional Christian not to worry about it too much. And because all my relationships with men have been very positive ones. I haven't known any kind of abusive relationship personally. What you see in Jesus is someone who is on your side, over and against all the religious bigots that are surrounding him. He is denouncing them and nurturing women. I don't see how one cannot but be drawn to that person.

But even when I have told stories about Jesus to women's groups and women outside the church, they have come back with different responses from the ones that I have on meeting this man. Some of them have felt the same. Some have warmed. Others have said, 'But we don't want to be in that position of dependence with a man. Why would we want to be vulnerable with a man?' And I think my answer to that is, 'Because every human being is vulnerable, and being vulnerable with someone you can trust is OK.' It is no loss of self-identity to be vulnerable. It actually puts you in touch with a greater dimension of your own worth than if you are always gritting your teeth and being self-sufficient.

Going back to what kind of relationship men have: I think Jesus invites them into vulnerability, and maybe some of them find that difficult to take on board. Whereas women have less to lose, in the cultural sense, because we have been there before.

MARGARET: Moving on from the psychological to the theological level: I ask myself, 'Why don't I find it a problem? Ought I to find it a problem? Is it of any relevance that Jesus was male? Could he have been female?' My theoretical answer is, 'The saviour of the world could equally have been female. It had to be a man or a woman, so there is no slighting of one or the other.' That's my theoretical answer, but the question is, 'Am I wholly convinced by it?'

ELAINE: Yes, that would be my answer, in that what we are talking about, theologically, is the Godhead becoming incarnate. All that relationality of the Trinity we were talking about takes on temporary human form. But there is no suggestion that the incarnation continues after Jesus' death: at that point we, the church, become the body of Christ, in a mystical kind of way.

MARGARET: This relates to a question I remember Sarah Coakley asking after a lecture: 'You don't think, do you, that after the resurrection Jesus was genitally male?' And I thought, 'Yes, I do.' We believe he rose, we believe he rose bodily – well then, what was his body like? We see people not recognizing him, but do you think on the road to Emmaus that figure could have been a woman?

ELAINE: No, I am sure that Jesus' resurrection appearances were as a man. I don't have any problems with that.

But where is Jesus now and what does he look like? That is a different question. I still do think of Jesus as a man. I am still stuck with the historical Jesus, not with a cosmic bit of the Trinity that has gone back to wherever it was before. So in that sense I have not lost the sense of the incarnation as a continuing thing, and in that sense I still focus on Jesus who was male.

MARGARET: I quite agree that the second person of the Trinity is neither male nor female. There is no sex in the pre-incarnate second person of the Trinity, the Word – *logos* (which is a male word) – or Wisdom – *sophia* (which is female). It is only in the incarnation that the maleness comes in.

But I wouldn't take the position that we have now gone back to where we were before. I would take the position that the historical Jesus is still alive with a resurrected body even though we are not having resurrection appearances.

What does the resurrection of the body mean? It means something that we don't quite know how to explain – except in the words of St Paul, 'it is sown a physical body, it is raised a spiritual body' (1 Corinthians 15:44) – but still there is a body there.

ELAINE: We all resurrect a body, and I have assumed that this body will be somehow non-sexual. Well, I have tried to think like that. 'In the resurrection they neither marry nor are given in marriage, but are like angels in heaven' (Matthew 22:30). But I don't know what it is to think of myself as non-female.

MARGARET: I certainly hope that, despite Jesus saying that, when I get to heaven I shall find I am married to Peter.

ELAINE: Did Christ have to be male? Did the incarnate Word have to be male? I think my answer is 'No'. God could have chosen to be incarnate in any form, but it only makes sense in human form, either male or female.

It would have been fairly pointless, logistically, for God to have come at that time as a woman. As a housewife some-where, it would have cut no ice! But it not only makes sense for God to come as a man, it reinterprets masculinity and maleness. For Jesus cut across a lot of stereotypes and taboos which are there in patriarchal cultures.

MARGARET: The arguments on the other side are that because God could choose the moment of the incarnation it is no use saying, 'In that culture he would have to be male,' because he could have chosen another culture and another time.

And I think the answer to that is, 'Important as the feminist issue is, it is not the only issue.' And Jesus was not obsessed by it: it was part of a wider battle for equality between human beings, of which sexual equality is only one element, among racial equality, and equality of the classes, and equality of people with disabilities, and more equalities which we probably haven't thought of yet in our society, struggling as we are with these sensitivities.

So it doesn't seem to me that he had to choose to express equality between the sexes in the fullest possible way, as though it was the number one issue.

ELAINE: There are a lot of questions there. 'Why did Jesus come as a Jew?' is also a significant question. If you believe in the historicity of God's relationship with the Jewish people, then that is incredibly significant. If you are sceptical about that, then it is another problem to resolve.

But because he came as a Jew, there are many things he did within the Jewish law and ritual that were clearly very significant. And they have stayed significant right through the centuries, in terms of our relationship with God. They raise questions about whether our relationship with God is defined by law-keeping or gift. Is it a relationship of legal justification or of grace?

In this significant moment in history, Christ was telling us something about God which is timeless and universal. Although it is said in the context of the Jewish people, the message of the love of God in Christ is inclusive of all contexts.

MARGARET: It is interesting making the parallel, isn't it, between the sexual question and the racial question. I would want to affirm the tradition of the Jews as the chosen people, in some sense. Maybe supremely chosen, because that was the race in which God chose to express the incarnation, but chosen also in that they had a particular understanding of the goodness and love of one God, as opposed to many gods.

Now I as a gentile can look to the Jews and say, 'You are the chosen people,' and feel happy that they are and I am not. The fact that gentiles have come in afterwards doesn't cause me any problem. But if you do that with male and female it does cause me a problem. I can't look at the male sex and say, 'You are the chosen sex, you know you are especially privileged.' It doesn't work that way. Why not?

ELAINE: That is a very good point. Why is it such an offence to do it that way and not an offence to do it the other way?

MARGARET: Maybe it is because of our guilt, because of the holocaust. But I am not sure it is that.

ELAINE: No, it is deeper than that. Is it because it is through that vehicle we are shown that God is a bigger God than anybody ever thought, and the gentiles really were incorporated from prophecies years before Christ? Maybe, again, it is something to do with our identity and our sexuality: our identity as gentiles is a very broad one. I don't know. I don't know why it doesn't work.

I have never thought of that before, Margaret. I feel perfectly secure in my relationship with God as a gentile, and I feel that if you understand Judaism properly then you understand that God loves the gentiles, and that the particularity of his love for the Jewish people doesn't in any sense isolate me or make me a second-class citizen.

But with the sexual thing – God particularly loves men, and Jesus became incarnate as a man, and it's only through men that we are received – that does something much deeper to my identity as a human being and as a woman. Because then it would mean I would have to go through men in order to get to Jesus, whereas I don't have to go through the Jews in order to get to God.

MARGARET: But we do go through the Jews to get to God.

ELAINE: But we only go through the Jews in that we go through Christ. We don't have to go through the law or through the Jewish people themselves.

MARGARET: Are you sure about that? We accept the Old Testament, and I think in a sense we have to become Jews in order to become Christians. Christianity is, after all, built on Judaism, and assimilating Judaism one understands Christianity better. You have to come at it from where Jesus was coming from. You can't cut off from that cultural, religious tradition. So in a sense I think we do have to come to Christ through Judaism. We don't do it enough.

ELAINE: I agree we go through the covenant that Judaism has given us, and the sacred writings of the scriptures: the commandments and the prophets. But not that we go through the observances, the law-keeping, the rituals and so on, because of all the things that Paul says about the law in Galatians ('If justification came through the law, then Christ died for nothing' Galatians 2:21). So, yes, we have to identify with the Jewish people at one level. But I wouldn't say we have to come through the Jewish people. I believe that is what Paul was arguing about right through Galatians and also in Acts 15 when he attacks circumcision for the gentiles.

MARGARET: Maybe we are talking about degrees. As you so rightly point out, we don't have to come through things like circumcision. That is all completely irrelevant now.

ELAINE: But to go back to our original point, it is interesting that there is no offence that Christ was a Jew and that God has a particular relationship with Jewish people, when it would be an enormous offence if God had a particular relationship with men.

MARGARET: I think this is why a lot of men cannot understand why we are offended, as women. They don't see why we feel it offensive for God to act particularly through men, and yet we do feel it offensive.

ELAINE: And it is offensive because they are men, not because they are cruel, nasty and vindictive men, or powerful and patriarchal men. It is because of the process more than because of the kind of men that they are.

It says something about our value as human beings. It demeans our image. Maybe that's it. If God has a special relationship with men that is almost saying that men are in the image of God, as the old fathers did, or some of them. Women just tag along as the reflections of men.

MARGARET: There is a letter in *The Tablet* this week that exactly points that out. Kevin Kelly writes: 'The fourth-century Ambrosiaster, who wrote strongly against the ordination of women, argued his case on the grounds that women were not made in the image of God. They were made in the image of man' (2 December 1995). Curious, isn't it?

There is a parallel question about black and white, if one calls Christ approximately white. Do black people find it any kind of a problem that Jesus was not black, at either a psychological or a theological level? I don't know.

ELAINE: Images are important. I remember having a chat with a North African woman who found the Aryan pictures of Jesus with golden locks, curly hair and a pale face very alienating. Some of her childhood had been in relation to these pictures in mission hospitals, and they had really turned her completely off. It wasn't until later, when she started to read the Gospels, she encountered a very different Christ. She said he was a dark-skinned Christ as far as she was concerned. He went through misunderstandings, misjudgements, clashes with authority, and so on. She found that the two were so different from each other that she was able to drop the Aryan image completely and go back to what she discovered in the New Testament.

MARGARET: Africans do the same thing as we women do with the scriptures. Simon of Cyrene is very important to them – an African who played such a key role.

ELAINE: And, of course, the early church was largely African, the church in Alexandria, which sent the missionaries out. We forget all that. There has been some interesting scholarship done recently about the church in the second century, or even earlier, being more black than it was white.

MARGARET: But in a way that raises the question: if it means so much to Africans that Simon of Cyrene came close to Jesus in carrying his cross, then wouldn't it mean so much more if Christ himself had been African?

The same question comes up with the women's issue: if it means so much to us that Mary Magdalene in the garden was the first Easter witness, then wouldn't it mean so much more to us if Christ himself had been female? And I don't know the answer to that.

ELAINE: For me I think the answer is: no, it wouldn't be any more positive. It isn't necessary. Also, as you suggested at the beginning, there is something about the maleness of Christ that is quite special for us, and possibly for a lot of women. Women right through the centuries have found the maleness of Christ certainly no stumbling block. Some have found it the opposite. It is not to do with their subordinate status, and wanting a hero on their side; but more to do with their recognition of intimacy, love and affirmation.

And maybe it's the same with the black Jesus issue. It's not so much that we need Jesus to be black or Jesus to be female, but we do need to hear from Jesus something very deep about what it means to be black or female. We need to know our worth and value and importance, through Christ's life, in God's vision for humanity.

I think that is why there is the black interest in Simon of Cyrene. As with women, there is an affinity with those people who share our characteristics who were close to Jesus. The fact that they gave something to Jesus is important. Jesus' vulnerability with women and his dependence on them is a tremendous plus for me. He presents to us a God who, in his incarnate life, is needy.

It is almost blasphemous in the evangelical tradition to suggest that God is needy. But Jesus needed the support of women, and of that strong African man to carry his cross. He receives from us at a level that says we are important, for if Jesus receives from us then our value is not in doubt. That is the significant factor for me, not the need for Jesus to be of my sex or my colour.

MARGARET: I think theologically the absolute rock and foundation of all this is *homo factus est*, which we lose in English: 'And he became man.' Well, 'man' has changed its meaning and that is now a mistranslation. It should be: 'And he became human.'

It is absolutely wonderful for me to know that the Creed says *homo factus est* and not *vir factus est*, which would mean, 'And he became man.'

ELAINE: With me, it was when I went to the Greek and realized the importance of that distinction between *anēr* – man – and *anthrōpos* – human being. It is such a simple thing. Just two Greek words. But for me it was a liberation, one of the changing moments for me – that sudden recognition that although I am not included in the *anēr*, I am included in the *anthrōpos*.

MARGARET: That's wonderful. And going along with that, the traditional doctrine – first formulated in rejection of the Apollinarian heresy in the fourth century – that what is not assumed is not redeemed. And therefore, going backwards, if we are redeemed then it is our humanity that is assumed. That is what the incarnation is about. That is the crucial point: that it is humanity that he took on, not maleness.

And that is the answer to all these people who go on about Jesus being a man. It is irrelevant that he was a man, because the doctrine of the church is, has always been, and I hope to God always will be, that the incarnation is God becoming human, and not God becoming man.

ELAINE: Yes, absolutely. I mean absolutely. That is the abiding reality. It goes beyond the historical particularity, which is cultural, ethnic, linguistic and gendered. But if we make theology out of the particularity then we lose the universal love of God anyway, and we are in danger of misunderstanding the meaning of the incarnation in its cosmic and eternal sense. So yes, I agree entirely.

MARGARET: The complication is that both *homo* and *anthrōpos*, although they clearly mean a human being of male or female sex, are male nouns. They came to be male nouns as a result of the fact that, at least up until the present age, the standard example of a human being has been a male one. Even if you draw a stick man it is a stick man that you draw. We have always culturally taken the man as being able to stand for man and woman.

You get this even more evidently in the Hebrew in Genesis, where *adam*, which is the equivalent of *anthrōpos* and *homo*, slides into becoming the male partner of the couple, Adam and Eve. And then the very point that one thought was being made by using *adam* rather than the Hebrew word that means man, *ish*, is lost when he becomes the male partner and you need another name for the female one.

The theological point should be clear, but one can see where the confusion creeps in.

Five

THE CHRISTA

MARGARET: People are really brought up, emotionally, against the question of whether it matters if Christ was male or female, when they look at a female crucified figure, which is often called a Christa. I have brought a number here.

How do you feel about crucifixes, coming from an evangelical background? Catholics are used to throwing crucifixes up all over the place, but your tradition doesn't put the figure on the cross, because he has risen.

ELAINE: Yes, that's true. Catholics have crucifixes, and Protestants have the empty cross. The wayside crucifixes throughout the Catholic parts of Europe have always felt more superstitious, to me, than Christian. Whereas the plain wooden crosses in Scandinavian churches have spoken eloquently of the victory of Christ's death and resurrection.

But I did begin to understand Catholic experience one summer in France. It was one of our family camping holidays and I think I was buying food in a village. It was pouring down with rain and I took shelter in the church. The church was in a terrible state. It had fallen into disuse and disrepair; abandoned, not used for worship any more. But it was still open. Waiting for the rain to stop, I sat in front of a crucifix left on a bare wall. There was something about its forlornness, its brokenness, in a church which was empty, desolate and deserted, that suddenly hit me in a completely new way. This really portrayed the Christ; the loneliness; the isolation; being rejected; allowing people to treat him that way; dying for us. And here the echo seemed to ring out, because these people too had abandoned Christianity. I was engaged in a moment of deep relationship with this figure represented on the cross. And I suddenly felt I understood something of what Catholics had been saying with their crucifixes all those years. This one spoke to me, unexpectedly, in an empty church, sheltering from the rain.

I still don't like too many crucifixes around, but I don't want to deny the value of that spiritual experience to other people. We miss so much if we don't contemplate the cross.

Let's look at what you've brought.

MARGARET: This is the first Christa I heard of, by Edwina Sandys. I read about it in 1984, when it was on display in the Cathedral of St John the Evangelist in New York. It is a very classic pose, just a female body instead of a male one. She has breasts and hips.

But this one is my favourite, from Toronto, in Canada. It was sculpted by Almuth Lutkenhaus in 1976. It's not called Christa, but *Crucified Woman*, so it doesn't even have to be seen as a female Christ. She said she set out not to do a religious work but to portray suffering. Which just goes to show that if you set out to portray suffering you do a religious work.

ELAINE: So why is it your favourite? Is it because the pose is beautiful? There isn't actually a cross there.

MARGARET: I gave a workshop with these two photographs of the same figure, one taken in the summer and one in the winter, and the participants pointed out that they bring out quite different aspects. Someone said that in the summer, with the tree behind and all its foliage, it is as though she is dancing on her tiptoes and holding out her arms in a beautiful pose. So that is a sort of resurrection crucifix. But in the winter the tree is bare, and she looks as though she has been stretched out to be raped. The same position can mean either of those things.

Both aspects are captured in the same crucifix (if we call it a crucifix), so you can see both the passion and resurrection, both the joy and the agony, depending on the season, or just on how you look at it. Artistically and theologically it is profound.

ELAINE: Yes, that is a very interesting difference.

MARGARET: It's also very sexual, isn't it? It's a woman who has been sexually abused. That hand points down at her sexual parts, and her legs are slightly apart. There is such pathos in it. She is very young as well, so it links up with child abuse.

ELAINE: The hands are very significant. In a certain sense the hand pointing down to herself is also almost maternal. That is what is ambiguous about it. On the one hand it is defeat, it is sorrow, it is almost self-protection, but at the same time it is a traditional pose of embrace, of inviting, of protecting. And the fact that the other hand is very different, I find very significant. Yes, the two couldn't be more different from the same statue, from the same angle. It is extraordinary.

MARGARET: And a bit of its history: it was shown at Bloor Street United Church, Toronto, at Easter 1979, and the reaction was then that it was obscene, blasphemous and heretical, mocking the basis of Christian religion. And Pastor Clifford said, defending it, that Christ represents all humanity, not just men, and people needed to see that message afresh. That is exactly what we finished the last chapter saying.

ELAINE: What is interesting is that it is not a crucifix, and it is not a Christa, but it is a woman crucified. It is quite easy to see that Christ represents all humanity including the woman, and you can see the identification of Christ in this woman, rather than that this woman is identified with Christ. Though the woman is representing Christ to us as well.

But it is slightly different from that one by Edwina Sandys, which is in the characteristic crucifix pose. Whereas this one isn't: there is no cross, the cross is only the shape of the woman's body, and it is clearly a portrayal of suffering, of naked anguish, suffering, defeat, brokenness, emptiness. It is the end of the defeat through rape and sexual violence. But with the beautiful tree behind it has the possibility of resurrection. In fact, she is almost beginning the dance of resurrection there.

Whereas the Edwina Sandys one doesn't have that same link with woman's torture, woman's violation, with woman's sexual vulnerability, at all. It is simply a female Christ, although the face is a broken and suffering face.

It is something to do with the religiousness of the shape and the depiction which gives this one a different sense. It is sad to hear people find it blasphemous, or in a sense debasing of Christ, because it is anything but that. It is for me an incredible depiction of the suffering of humanity and of women, particularly women, that took Christ to the cross. The sins that we suffer, and some people far more than others, that is all part of Christ and the sacrifice.

MARGARET: The other bit of history about the Toronto one is that in December 1989 there was a famous murder in Canada, when a man called Marc Lepine, who had been refused a place as an engineering student, went into a university in Montreal with a gun and murdered fourteen women engineering students. He just called the women out and shot them because they were women. And he said afterwards: 'I have decided to send the feminists who have always ruined my life to their maker.' And, 'The feminists have always enraged me, they want to keep the advantages of women … while seizing for themselves those of men.'

After that, when people were very shocked and stunned, a group gathered in front of this *Crucified Woman* at Emmanuel College, and there were bouquets of flowers, red roses and carnations, and they passed round a crystal chalice of red wine. That is actually what the crucifixion is meant to be telling us: how Christ suffers the worst of the agonies that we go through, and how he is brought to the worst debasement that is possible.

You hear stories of how particular women, especially those who have been raped, find tremendous healing when they can identify what happened to them with the crucifixion. We allow them to feel like that, as long as it is not portrayed artistically.

ELAINE: Yes, that is very interesting. I remember the first time I came across this, I was quite young, I don't think I had been a Christian very long, and I was reading a book by someone who was a well-known evangelical medical missionary at that time. She had been working in Kenya when the Mau Mau terrorists broke in, and they raped her. She described it in this book and it was horrendous to read. Suddenly, in the middle of an account of prayer and missionary work, there is this rape. But she finds herself thinking of Christ's suffering, even during the rape and torture itself.

She talked about the brutality of the men. She was a woman who had never had sexual relationships, and her only experience of sex was so brutalizing and violent, without any tenderness or gentleness. And, in the middle of it all, she feels that Christ is there suffering with her, in the rape. It was the only thing that kept her sane in the situation. Christ was saying, 'I am with you, they are doing this to me as well as to you.' She describes it in such a powerful way.

I found the account profoundly shocking and remember it even now, although it must have been thirty years since I read it. The shock was that this strait-laced missionary lady could talk about rape and bring Christ into that event and experience his love as healing. But I have reflected on it many times since. And I have heard that same story in many different ways from women who have undergone sexual violence.

MARGARET: You have heard it many times?

ELAINE: Yes, not that they thought about this at the time, but part of their healing has been in recognizing that Christ suffered the same kind of debasement, and that there is healing through Christ's own suffering.

MARGARET: That is the real question, isn't it? There it is, posed in a pastoral, meditational form. Is it valid for a woman to say, 'Christ was in me, in that they were doing it to him'?

One can say, 'Yes it is valid, and this is the incarnation.' But if you say, 'No, the maleness of Christ is essential,' then it is only in some indirect sense that you can talk of a similarity, and there is not an identity there.

I suppose some of the opponents of women's ordination, or opponents of Christian feminism, would want to reject the way she wrote about it. Probably most would accept it, but would draw the line at putting it in pictorial form, in a crucifix.

Also relevant to this is the trouble in Bavaria recently over the crucifixes they have in school. One of the pupils objected, and said: 'I find it disturbing when I am doing my lessons to have this image over my head of a naked man pouring blood.' Now the church reaction has been to say, 'How appalling of her to object, what a silly reaction. We are going to have crucifixes, everyone will have to accept it.'

But in a sense, although the conclusion of removing crucifixes was wrong, there was value in her saying that she finds it shocking. Because when we don't find a crucifix shocking, it has been emptied of its meaning.

I want to hold on to the shock value of the crucifix as well as the right to have quite a lot of crucifixes around. But I don't think we should have them around so much that we lose the shock value. And, of course, the shock value is there in a much magnified form if it is a naked woman instead of a naked man.

Yet, while you get crucifixes that show the horror, there are also crucifixes that show Christ very evidently risen and crucified at the same time. I think it is a mistake to see the crucifix as identifying with the pre-resurrection. It can throw the emphasis on the passion, or it can throw the emphasis on the glorification.

In this wonderful instance, called the Gómez Cross, from El Salvador, both death and resurrection are evoked. This is the sort of Christa (though it is not called a Christa) that even a male chauvinist could find acceptable, because the association of the woman with Christ on the cross is so subtle that it is not going to offend anyone.

This cross was made in memory of a woman, Maria Cristina Gómez, who was actually killed. She was an active member of the Baptist Church and a primary school teacher, and took part in discussions about justice. In April 1989 she was abducted in a van with darkened windows, and her body was later dumped: she had acid burns on her back and had been shot four times.

So, in that sense, this cross has the real meaning of the crucified one. Yet what you see is a peasant woman with patches on her garments stretching out her hands in joy. It is a great celebration of work. It is very much an incarnation crucifix, even a pre-passion crucifix, because here God is found in all the activities of work that women do – ploughing the field, picking the berries, nursing the baby, teaching at school.

ELAINE: Two teaching figures – one in the open air and one with the blackboard. And each of them has something powerfully celebratory about it. That ploughing the field has a wonderful sun, and the bird has the connotations of the dove, and so on. A real burst of colour at the top there. And feeding the baby outside on this rock as this chirpy yellow bird is tweeting away, with a lovely cactus in bloom. And there is another beautiful cactus that has just burst into bloom with a single red flower. Very moving, that one. And next to it the woman with her arms outstretched, who moves in and out of three or four of the images. I think there is a tremendous celebration about all of them. It is a profound piece of work.

MARGARET: It reminds me of a very Catholic devotional tradition, the morning offering, which offers all the prayer, work, sufferings and joys of the day to God. So the offering of all those things becomes taken up into the total self-offering of Christ, which of course is the cross.

ELAINE: It is a very happy picture, isn't it? It is a picture about resurrection and celebration.

MARGARET: Yet done in memory of a woman who had been murdered. Here's another Christa, called *Das weibliche Antlitz Gottes* ('The female image of God'), by an Indian artist, Lucy D'Souza, in 1990. The crucified figure is both a woman and a tree. How do we know it is a woman? Well, breasts and belly and long hair. And she is flanked by four women who symbolize earth, water, air and fire, or the compassion, kindness, wisdom and shining presence of God. And there is this great tangle of roots at the bottom of the tree...

ELAINE: ...with figures in the roots who could be human babies.

MARGARET: Yes, seeing them as babies makes it more womblike. Now, I understand that although this was commissioned as a hunger cloth by Missio, the German missionary agency, they couldn't use it for the purpose they had intended because of the potential offence.

When I gave a workshop on the Christa, just over a year ago, at the Catholic Theological Association, one of most articulate Catholic women said that she had always taken the view that you simply could not use the Christa in mixed male–female workshops because reactions were so emotive.

ELAINE: I know men who would relate positively to this but they are not typical.

MARGARET: The objection people always bring to the Christa is to say, 'But Jesus wasn't a woman, you are changing it.' But you can put a negro Christ on the cross and as long as he is male, nobody minds. Make it a woman and people are tearing their hair out.

Now this is the most shocking one, this *Bosnian Christa* by Margaret Argyle. It was done in memory of the women raped in Bosnia. I wonder how you relate to that? I don't know if you remember reading in the press about a liturgy in Manchester Cathedral in October 1993 for the Ecumenical Decade of Churches in Solidarity with Women, where there was a Christa figure? This is the one. You are not shocked? I have spoken to people who were at the liturgy and didn't find it at all shocking, but quite moving.

ELAINE: I don't find it moving, either.

MARGARET: It is very sexual. These curtain-like bits are like the labia, with that point at the top as the clitoris, and then of course it is blood red inside. It is all made out of fabric.

ELAINE: So all this is embroidered? And how is the figure made, then?

MARGARET: Maybe it is just outlined with some very fine stitching. But the objection in the press was not that it was sexual, but that it had a female figure. You see the suggestion of breasts? Shock, horror, a gasp of fury: 'They paraded around a woman on the cross.' But talking to the person who was at the liturgy, it sounded as though in the context of the occasion the congregation was with it. It worked.

ELAINE: For me, I wouldn't want this anywhere near worship. It is an interesting idea, and has aesthetic and intellectual significance. It is a sombre statement of something 'other', mysterious, hidden, traditionally female; it is not easily understandable. But if it was carried round in a church it wouldn't engage me. Nor, I think, would it shock me or horrify me; it would just be irrelevant in terms of worship. I can see how some of these others are much more appropriate to worship and some speak at a deeper level, but this wouldn't do anything at all.

MARGARET: I have exactly the same responses as you. Clearly the Salvadorean one and the Canadian one are both aids to prayer in different ways. It is a traditional Catholic practice to pray to Christ on the cross. St Ignatius, for example, had a famous prayer to Christ on the cross, asking himself what he had done for Christ, what he was doing for him, and what he was going to do for him.

And I remember Cardinal Hume saying once that when he was feeling very low, he would pick up his crucifix and kiss the feet of Christ crucified. That is not the way everyone prays but it is the way some people pray, and I think there is something profound about it.

But is it the same to talk to Christ on the cross, with a female figure as a visual aid? I don't know the answer to that. If everything I have said about it is true, then it should not make a difference.

Or are we going back to the beginning of our previous conversation, when I was saying perhaps it does make a difference, but in some ways it is a positive difference? Is it the same Christ that one prays to if the figure is a female one?

The truth is, I think, one uses the Christa figure, not to pray to directly, but as a spur to prayer in some other way. For example, with this Salvadorean cross, to pray in thankfulness and praise and self-offering. This one says to me, 'I take my work – which is woman's work out in the fields – and I offer it to you; and I offer it along with the offering of Christ on the cross.' That's the way I look at it.

ELAINE: But also it says to me that you can do what you like to us at the end of the day, you can even murder us, but there is victory beyond, because of our resurrected, crucified Christ who gives meaning to the whole of life and death. That's incredibly profound, knowing why that was done and in whose memory. I mean, that grows on me the more I look at it. It is just exciting. So it is victory out of what could have been the most horrendous defeat. And it is celebration out of brokenness and death and, I suppose, resurrection. It is all of those together.

MARGARET: But it works because I look there and I place myself there. That is what we are called to do when we look at a crucifix, to place ourselves with Christ on the cross. So it does not have to be a question of talking to the figure on the cross. That is not what one is doing, but one is placing oneself with the figure there in order to be close. That is different.

ELAINE: And that is an emphasis that we never had in Protestantism or in the Church of England – placing yourself on the cross with Christ. It has been the other way round. It definitely is Christ on the cross, not you, but you would have been there if it weren't for Christ, and so there is always a distance, a thankfulness that this is something that Christ has taken on alone and that we could never do.

So our worship is the worship of thankfulness rather than identification. That is why, when I have read some of the women who have found this an enormous struggle, I have had to work quite hard to enter into that. It is not part of my own spiritual experience, or hasn't been for all these years.

Six

SACRIFICE

ELAINE: Sacrifice, atonement and blood are key issues today for feminists. To what extent does the atonement through Christ's sacrificial blood liberate women? Does it free us to become full participants in the Reign of God? Or does it idealize women's suffering and women's victim status?

There are those feminist theologians who argue that it is the latter rather than the former, suggesting that atonement language employs symbols which reinforce the image of God as a vengeful, mirthless, wrathful, dominating, male deity, demanding payment for the fact that he has been disobeyed, and sentencing his only Son to a violent death. So God is brutal rather than compassionate: in fact, the US feminist Mary Daly argues that concepts like expiation, blood sacrifice, condemnation and guilt offering portray God as sado-masochistic, and Christianity as a necrophilic religion centred around a dead man on a cross. She, along with other post-Christian feminists, also alleges that traditional atonement theories steal concepts from women's experiences. Bodily brokenness, rape, defilement have all become glorified in the person of Christ, but these belong to women. So the church romanticizes and idealizes suffering which women have experienced as barbaric and awful.

MARGARET: That is a very good articulation of the feminist critique.

ELAINE: It's summed up in the statement in Mary Grey's book *Redeeming the Dream* (SPCK, 1989, p. 118), that from being the means of liberation, 'identifying with the sufferings of Jesus on the Cross, held up as essential for redemption, has contributed to woman remaining transfixed as victim and scapegoat in society'. And Mary Daly says something quite similar, in *Beyond God the Father* (The Women's Press, 1986, p. 77): 'It is significant that it is not only the negative qualities of a victim that have been projected upon women: the propensity for being temptresses, the evil and matter-bound "nature" of the female, the alleged shallowness of mind, weakness of will, and hyper-emotionality.' Mary Daly really loves this stuff. 'The qualities that Christianity idealizes, especially for women, are also those of the victim, sacrificial love, passive acceptance of suffering, humility, meekness, etc. Since these are the qualities idealized in Jesus "who died for our sins", his functioning as a model reinforces the scapegoat syndrome for women.' That is really trying to shape up the issue.

MARGARET: Yes.

ELAINE: Now, although I hear this case and see its weight from their perspective, I feel curiously untouched by the argument.

MARGARET: That's absolutely fascinating because I was going to say exactly the same thing. Why do I not react like those other women to it? Why do I find it so marvellous when they find it so awful?

People like Mary Grey hate it. Here is another quote from her in *Redeeming the Dream*, when she says redemption 'has overtones which ring of suffering, sacrifice, guilt and self-negation, the negativity of the cross of Jesus Christ and the severity of the atonement doctrines which try to explain it'. But it's not just Mary Grey, it's almost a consensus isn't it?

This one would be an interesting one to explore together, because I would have thought that my love of the sacrifice of the Mass, and the blood of Christ, is very much to do with my Catholicism. And you are presumably coming at it from a different place.

ELAINE: That's right, that's why I think this discussion is very fruitful. I would have expected for us to differ on this, because Protestantism has never really highlighted the idea of women suffering with Christ. But there is a tradition within Catholicism of being caught up in Christ's suffering and passion, both in meditation and in a physical way. I know flagellation and self-mutilation are aberrations within Catholicism, but they are there, whereas they are quite absent in evangelicalism. So although my reaction is to be expected, I am a little surprised that it doesn't touch you.

MARGARET: Obviously it touches Mary Grey, who is a Catholic. If I am to say why I think it is marvellous, then I think of paintings. The one I have most in mind is in the English College in Rome, a great piece behind the altar: the Father lifts up the dead body of his Son, and as he is lifting it, it forms a crucified shape. I find the idea that this is a brutal, vengeful God inflicting punishment on his Son superficial. This is the terrible agony of the parent holding a dead child, and yet somehow knowing at the same time that this is necessary.

What makes it necessary for justice is not an arbitrary rule of God, it's something almost bigger than God. I do feel to some extent the idea that justice must be satisfied, and we can see that society feels that too, for example when people talk about Myra Hindley. The argument against her release is that what she has done is so terrible that it can never be made up for. And this is where the Christian faith comes home with such triumph and compassion. Of course she can't make up for it: no number of years in prison, no number of times being banned from riding ponies or whatever, can make the slightest difference to what she has done. But in a metaphysical way it has been made up for. And therefore, of course, she can be released.

ELAINE: I would agree entirely with that. Our own legal system can only deal with cases and prescribe punishment. It cannot handle the ultimate questions of justice. But Christ's redemptive suffering does. It addresses the need for the satisfaction for guilt required by the very moral structure of the universe: a structure put in place, or course, by God. And Christ's atonement also means there is an end to our punishment. Through him, things have been dealt with, concluded. As evangelicals say a lot: 'The price has been paid.' But only at a cost. That's why I think the picture of a bereaved father is much more appropriate than that of a vengeful deity. It says God is prepared to go to this length for the sake of love and justice.

MARGARET: Sacrifice and suffering and punishment and guilt, these are all tremendously deep notions. They touch on Greek tragedy and the notion of catharsis. All that is very powerful.

One can begin to understand it even without going through an extreme example like Myra Hindley. I suppose we all ought to feel the need all the time of not being able to make up for our sins, but the fact is most of us don't feel that very acutely. But one can imagine feeling it. For example, say I were to drive without putting my glasses on (I've no idea actually whether I would pass the required test, but the fact is I wouldn't be driving in optimum conditions) and supposing I had one of my children in the car, and I killed her. How could I ever forgive myself? I don't know.

If I could, it would only be through being able to say, 'There is no way I can ever make up for this but someone else has made up for it on my behalf. I can be at peace, because someone else has taken that burden up without belittling the crime.' That's the point, isn't it? What the parents say about Myra Hindley is that if you let her out, you belittle the crime.

ELAINE: That is because there is no redemptive thinking within the Myra Hindley debate, except for occasional comments from Christian people. Otherwise everything is couched in totally punitive terms.

But going back to the feminist question, how do we respond to Carter Heyward? She argues that positing this Other to take guilt on our behalf is counter-productive. We end up looking for a hero figure rather than standing on our own feet and accepting our own responsibilities. It also lets men off the hook, because they can dump everything on this superman-hero and not face up to things themselves.

MARGARET: The fact is that this hero figure is indeed my hero figure. He has taken that guilt off me, not in some theoretical, mathematical, out-there sort of way, but through love and through suffering. If we can take that in at all, it leaves us wrung out like a rag, so we are transformed.

The thought that someone else, out of love for us, should have sacrificed his life, is something terrifying. It is not taking the responsibility off us, it is putting us through the rack of saying – like the alcoholic – 'I need help and I can't help myself.' It is that cry for help, in this case a cry to God for help, which is transforming.

ELAINE: Another thing many feminists don't like is the way the church has used Christ's death to reinforce women's guilt. Atonement is necessary because women are guilty: the Church Fathers implied that women have a particular responsibility for sin. As Tertullian said: 'You are the devil's gateway. It was because of you Christ had to die.' The Victorians implied the opposite: that we expect sin of men, but when women are evil it is unpardonable, because women should stand for purity and goodness (the Myra Hindley case again). Whichever way you look at it, feminists have some justification for their allegation that women have been treated differently over the issue of sin. Men are forgiven their sins more easily than women.

MARGARET: Yes, I agree with that. I agree that there is a justified case in saying that the theology of the cross has been used in a way that has sometimes been destructive for women. What you say about women being more blamed, carrying more of the guilt, has a lot to do with the fact that preachers have been men. As men they are more aware of the way that women let them down than of the way that their own sex lets down women. That is part of the reason, maybe the whole reason, I don't know.

There is the phenomenon that is so often alluded to, that in the past an unfaithful woman was a terrible slut and a whore, whereas it was expected that a man would need other experiences to satisfy him.

But as well as women bearing the greater guilt, another aspect is that the identification of their suffering with Christ,

the carrying of their cross daily, would mean forgiving a husband seventy times seven, in, for example, a battered-wife
situation. Living through that has been seen as her way of
finding redemption.

It doesn't need to be as extreme as being physically battered, but it happens in all the ways in which women have
been emotionally limited, or just restricted – through being
confined to the home, through financial restrictions. This has
all been seen as part of carrying your cross.

ELAINE: To make it even worse, there are also people who
have spiritualized religious suffering in such a way that it has
given them almost a spiritual high. One of my worst experiences was hearing a male priest, a Catholic priest, in a group
I meet with regularly. He was a newcomer to the group and
didn't stay for more than a few weeks because he was asked to
leave. But at one key point he described the painting of the
rape of the Sabine women as exquisitely beautiful. Looking at
the painting gave him a spiritual high because he thought
those women really enjoyed the torture and the rape. He
could see something sensually pure and enjoyable in the
women luxuriating in this torture, which reminded him of
Christ's suffering, and brought him to a heightened spiritual
awareness.

You can imagine what that did to the rest of the group!
It sent shivers down the spines of the women, and, of course,
most of the men found it very hard to cope with. But what
came out in the discussions that followed was that this wasn't
an experience unique to him. There is apparently almost
a tradition in some male spirituality of glorifying women's
sexual suffering, and identifying it with Christ. I think that is
what a lot of feminists are recoiling against, with very good
justification.

MARGARET: It is fascinating hearing you tell that story, because half an hour ago I was making a call from a phone box in the heart of Mayfair, and I could hardly stand in the box, it was so disgusting. An entire wall with prostitute cards, but the terrifying thing was that it was not just straight prostitution. Every one was sado-masochism, every one. Dozens of them, with the most terrifying little drawings.

Well, that is what this Catholic priest is talking about, isn't he? How men like to inflict suffering on a woman and fantasize that she is enjoying it.

ELAINE: There is the idea that women enjoy suffering because it brings them in touch with Christ, so you have a theological justification for allowing them to suffer, even for inflicting it.

However, I don't think that all of this touches the deep, theological point about the inclusiveness of Christ's sacrifice. Christ died for all of us, men and women equally, and there is nothing at the heart of the Christian faith which permits us to make any distinctions between women and men with regard to sinfulness. If the church has, even unwittingly, done this, it in no sense deflects from Christ's work. We shouldn't blame God for the wrong emphasis the church has given.

MARGARET: Is there anything more that you can say about the atonement? The other week I had dinner with some very good theologians, and the Anselm idea of substitution came up. They all absolutely took it for granted that no one today could have any truck with such an appalling theology. Yet I think Anselm is marvellous.

ELAINE: Substitutionary atonement is what evangelicals have always emphasized. It is fundamental to our whole understanding of the centrality of the cross, so I am delighted that you think Anselm is marvellous in this! But why did they take it for granted that it was passé?

MARGARET: Precisely because of the case you outlined, the vengeful father demanding the sacrifice of his son. Can you say anything about why you are not disturbed by the vengeful father demanding the sacrifice of his son?

ELAINE: I'll try. First, the presentation is wrong. It is not just a matter of God the Father vindicating his own will. It is that love and righteousness go together. They are there at the heart of the universe, so evil matters and cannot go unpunished; wrong has to be righted. We are being brought face to face here with the horror of sin. Sin shouldn't be shrugged off or 'normalized'. The way that we treat one another, the way that we live in this world, matters enormously. Even the smallest belittling or humiliating unkindness matters, because it is adding to the whole pool of human misery.

But the atonement says that God takes the punishment personally, out of love. The structure of love is costly for all of us. Anyone who loves is open to pain and suffering. And for the sins of humankind there is nobody else who can actually give what it costs, because nobody else has that amount of love to give except for God. God is prepared to go through that suffering, to this extent, for the sake of human beings. I agree with those who say it is a great mystery, but I disagree with those who find it sinister. The Father is not characterized by his vengeance, but by his love.

And then, I believe we have to see atonement as trinitarian. This is not a senior deity punishing a junior one, or a Father God needing to scapegoat the Son God to appease his anger. It is a decision and an act of the Trinity together.

In some way which we cannot understand, the eternal Trinity willingly undertakes an act of separation for our redemption. Therefore Christ's suffering is as much an initiating act of the Son (although the Son wrestles with it, because he suffers it as a human being) as it is an act of the Father. There is not a hierarchy of Being at the heart of the Godhead. That is a conclusion we come to in error, when we read the earthly Christ's relationship with the Father back into the eternal Trinity.

So Christ's sacrifice is very sombre and breathtaking, but it is not vengeful or spiteful. The reality of it brings you more into contact with who you are and the weight of sin in the world. It challenges us to recognize just what we are taking on when we sin.

MARGARET: Yes, I agree with all that. And when you talk of the little sins, the belittling words, I think we do actually feel the gravity of belittling words. A chance remark or thoughtless comment can leave a real wound that festers, particularly at a vulnerable time. And it does take a lot to heal these things. So it is not just theoretical. Sin is very grave. When we suffer it we hurt. When our child is hit by a drunken driver, then we really feel the gravity of it.

On sacrifice. 'Sacrifice' obviously is a word that sets off negative associations for many women, which is exactly what Mary Grey was saying in her quote. But it doesn't for me, and I am a little puzzled by it, because it seems to me such a universal part of human experience that you do sacrifice for those you love. It is almost the way that you know you love someone: you find yourself willingly doing without for their sake, or you find yourself surprised by how much their suffering hurts you too.

So sacrifice is not some cultic concept out of the blue that we have to be argued into accepting. It is the whole beauty and rhythm of the universe. It's love that makes the world go round. Everyone sacrifices.

ELAINE: In Christianity you don't have a picture of the gods requiring human sacrifice, as in a lot of religious mythology. Usually, it is the gods that have to be vindicated and human beings who have to suffer. Christianity offers a very different scenario, of God who suffers on our behalf. God takes the lead in sacrifice, rather than exacting it somehow from us. Because human life is so sacred and important, so central, we would do anything rather than give it up. But God does give life up. And that is for me a very challenging concept, an incredibly humbling one.

MARGARET: I have a slight difficulty over that. What's the name of that theology that says God suffers – process theology? I think that to believe in a God who actually suffers is somehow denying the nature of God, the omnipotence of God. So the suffering of God I would take in a more figurative sense.

I have spoken of how I am moved by the pictures of the grieving Father holding his dead Son – the other side of the coin of the Pieta with Mary holding her dead Son – and yet somehow the suffering is done because God can't suffer. God has to become incarnate in order to suffer. If I'm denying that God in his or her divine nature actually suffers, I would also be denying that God in his or her divine nature stands there in a cool, impassive way at these horrors.

But somehow the suffering bit of God is in Christ, and that is why Christ has to be human. But insofar as we speak of God in an anthropomorphic sense it is good to talk about God walking in the garden in the cool of the day, and God thinking and feeling and all sorts of things, but not to understand them literally. Because somehow that makes God less than God.

ELAINE: So does God have no feelings? I see your point, but I'm not sure, I don't know.

MARGARET: I want to say that God is not unfeeling, but perhaps God has no feelings in the strict literal sense. What are feelings when they apply to God?

ELAINE: I can understand how God cannot be at the mercy of anything like human feelings. Our suffering tosses us about and often throws us off course, so I can understand why you wouldn't want to apply that to God. But I think I still want to talk in some sense of suffering in relation to God.

MARGARET: There is another reason why I want to pull back from that process language. God is omnipotent, but God is less of a comfort and salvation to me if, in burying myself in God, I cannot find total peace. God is total peace. If I am throwing myself into the arms of someone who is actually upset himself, that's not much of a heaven.

ELAINE: I would agree entirely, and yet in order to throw yourself into the arms of God, you have to be confident that God understands who you are and how you need to receive peace. This is then back to the early feminist question: how can a male Christ understand women, or a male Christ save us? What they mean, I suppose, is how can anything that is male get inside the psyche and emotions of women?

And my answer to that has always been: 'Because Christ suffered'. There is something about the sufferings of Christ that means we come to a God who is compassionate and all-knowing, not simply because he is an omniscient deity, but because he has entered into human experience. So God knows my suffering, pain, grief, without being knocked off course by it. I suppose I always want it both ways.

People have a logical problem with the idea of Christ being both human and divine. But from a Christian point of view, he was 'both-and'. In him, divine authority and human responsibility hold together. God's foreknowledge and human freedom is another 'both-and'. So is the need to hold together time and eternity; we don't know what we mean when we talk in temporal terms about God, because there isn't any time there. Much of Christian theology is built on 'both-and' rather than 'either/or'. Perhaps in that sense, too, God has suffered, and experienced grief, but God is also perfect peace.

MARGARET: I think we are touching on something quite important. It is just clarifying in my mind. Why the incarnation and why the mystery of the two natures? How can that be? God needs to be incarnate in order to share our suffering, because otherwise you have the distance of the God beyond our suffering. God has got to be human in order to suffer. We need him to suffer.

But he has got to be divine in order to be the perfect peace where there is total salvation, the place where suffering is no more. If God is not the place where suffering is no more, then he's not much help to us.

But if God doesn't suffer with us he is not much help to us either. That is why we need the incarnation. Both-and.

ELAINE: I liked the way you put that. It's certainly what I think. I wonder if I can make it more concrete? As you know, I do quite a lot of work with incest survivors. You get a group of women who are suffering pain now because of what happened years ago: it is physical pain and sexual pain, it's vilification, it's violation, defilement. Now the radical feminist critique sees Christ as utterly irrelevant in terms of being able to help. His maleness links him with the abusers. But this is why I think this feminist critique is fundamentally wrong. Because the women I know who have actually been able to approach Christ in their pain have found there somebody who was also defiled, treated barbarically, humiliated physically and sexually; someone people spat at, who was trussed up with no clothes on, and in his torture presumably urinating down the cross. It must have been horrendous, you know, the sheer bodily torment that they made him endure.

And this God – in whom there is no more grief or pain – has actually gone through this. In the end that is the only real thing I can offer women who are struggling with memories of incest and their own worthlessness: that God knows what this means, and ultimately there is hope and peace in this God. And I know many women who found that, because they have been able to realize that God understands.

But your point is so important, and I hadn't put it into words myself; that at the same time they need somebody who is not crying and weeping now, not struggling now. There is a need for God to be the one who can surround them with love and say, 'It's all right, there is peace here.'

MARGARET: Father or mother. Parent. Are you always able to offer this to your incest victims, I wonder, to people who are not Christian?

ELAINE: That is very hard. Sometimes the incest has taken place within the context of the hands of the church, which makes that very, very hard. When people who are supposed to represent God have done this, what does that say about God? That he is on the side of the abuser, the malefactor, the torturer?

So I understand why many of the feminist writers are very angry, especially if they have come into contact with the pain of the women that I have. It is a terrible thing, but it is a result of human sin, not God. At the end of the day one has to say that.

There are very few women who can hear the truth of this, but whenever I get the opportunity I do say it. It is important for healing that this is let go of.

MARGARET: That's what that Canadian crucifix that we looked at last time, that's what that says.

ELAINE: I have been looking at a lot more crucifixes since we had that last talk.

MARGARET: There are some more things I want to say about blood. Some years ago, a programme called *Through the Devil's Gateway* (Channel 4, 10 October 1989) introduced some new ideas to me on menstruation and the symbolism of salvation through blood. I wrote a little thing about it at the time, which was not published because I gave it to *The Tablet* and the editor said it would be going too far. But I'll run through the ideas that came up, because they are quite interesting.

The programme said that Hindu women have to stay outside the 'circle of purity', that includes the kitchen, to the point where pans that have been washed up by a menstruating woman would have to be washed up again by someone else. Jewish women go through a purifying bath after menstruation before they can have sexual relations again. Christian women are told they cannot consecrate the sacrificial blood of the redeemer. And until quite recently in the Catholic Church they could not get too close to it by serving at the altar.

There is somebody called Penelope Shuttle, who wrote a book called *The Wise Wound* (HarperCollins, 1994), and she said on this programme: 'The reason that it is so difficult for religious hierarchies and authorities to take on board the menstrual experience is that – let us take the Christian example – it is uncomfortably close to what is happening in the church ritual.' She explained, 'It is women each month who experience the sacrifice of a possible child, experience the flow of blood, experience this in a sacramental way and are themselves reborn from it. This is the very thing that churches say happens with a male God. But it doesn't happen to men, it happens to women.'

The Hindu comparison came from Sanjukta Gupta. She explains that in Hinduism, 'every god has a power, which is his wife', and 'the power is the basis of continuing the universe – the fertility, the life and death and everything – and men haven't got it, they have to borrow it'.

And then a Jewish scholar called Leonie Archer talked about circumcision, and said that circumcision was not just the severing of the foreskin but the flowing of blood. And she said: 'Women bleed naturally, passively, uncontrollably, part of the life-giving cycle of nature. Men by one act enact a cultural re-birth.' She is talking about circumcision. 'They impose themselves upon their bodies and they bleed culturally.'

And then I reflected on Julian of Norwich, who talks about the bleeding of Jesus as a way of seeing him as mother.

ELAINE: I had not put that together. Yes, of course.

MARGARET: At least, she sees the cross as labour, it is not so much menstruation. 'He carries us within him in love and travail, until the full time when he wanted to suffer the sharpest thorns and cruel pains that ever were or will be.' (*Showings*, chapter 60).

ELAINE: I found the article by Leonie Archer compelling. She also argues for the high status of the issue of male blood (circumcision) compared with the low status of the issue of female blood (menstruation).

MARGARET: So when there is this tremendous sensitivity about the woman priest, this is all linked up.

ELAINE: Oh, yes, I think so. There is a true story, which has now become a legend, about a woman who was on the short-list to be deacon at a cathedral, and the big question for the men who were interviewing was: 'What happens if she becomes pregnant?' The idea of a sexually active woman with a full belly administering the sacraments was horrendous. And they weren't satisfied with the answer, 'Well, she'll have a baby.'

Blood and life, sexuality and spirituality, are so uncomfortably close.

MARGARET: Penelope Shuttle was interesting on the spirituality of menstruation when she said this monthly bleeding is the sacrifice of a possible child and women are reborn through it. It's a purifying, and a starting again.

ELAINE: Yes. But it has always been a shame and an embarrassment, something that you keep out of view in the church, as it was in Judaism.

I used to be curious to know why an Orthodox rabbi, whom I knew reasonably well, never shook my hand. I asked a Jewish friend why this should be the case, and he said, 'Oh, it's quite simple, you might be menstruating.'

MARGARET: Gosh. In Orthodox Judaism, do women proclaim where they are in their cycle so everyone can know if they can be touched?

ELAINE: I doubt it. It isn't something I usually discuss! They probably just avoid the possibility by not touching a woman at all. A friend of mine who knows this rabbi very well is quite naughty: she always goes towards him with her hand outstretched, so he has to put his hand in his pocket or whistle.

One of my favourite miracles is when Jesus heals the menstruating woman (Luke 8). His attitude is so different from that of the surrounding culture. Even though the woman should not be in the crowd and certainly not touching his clothing, that is not the issue for him. When he forces her into the open to admit what has happened, the issue for him is that she has taken the initiative in faith. I find that remarkable.

MARGARET: She has asked for help.

ELAINE: Yes, that's right. And he commends her actions, even though technically they are defiling him, because she has believed and approached him. Her faith released Christ's power to make her whole. It's incredibly powerful.

MARGARET: That's a wonderful biblical refutation of the idea of menstrual pollution.

Another aspect of menstruation that is sacrificial is the discomfort of period pains.

But then there is the idea that men have borrowed the idea of sacrificial, life-giving blood and made it something cultic.

And to enable them to take over this blood that gives life, they have to keep women out of it, so that this is the male life-giving blood and not the female one.

But what I don't like about this is any kind of implication, if there is one, that there is a wicked male conspiracy.

ELAINE: Yes, that's right, that's what makes one uneasy about it.

MARGARET: Yet the opponents of women's ordination are the first to say that there are very deep typologies in the male and female, which we cannot altogether plumb. They have religious implications, they say, and we play around with them at our peril.

ELAINE: Quite.

MARGARET: And in a sense they are right.

ELAINE: Yes.

MARGARET: But because they are right, that is actually why we need women priests so badly. Let's make that our next conversation.

Seven

PRIESTHOOD

ELAINE: Is priesthood predominantly linked with the Eucharist for you?

MARGARET: Definitely, because that is the priestly action. But then it isn't a priestly action for you, is it?

ELAINE: No, it isn't. I spent a lot of time worshipping in Brethren Assembly because my parents-in-law were Brethren, and there not only do you have no priests, but anyone may celebrate at any time during the Lord's Table (which is the name of the Eucharist).

We would sit in a circle round a table on which there were the elements – it is rather like a Quaker service but without the silence and with general participation – and at some stage a man would get up and walk over to the table and read a relevant passage of scripture and begin to celebrate. And then another or the same man would take the wine, and so on. Now, of course, it is inclusive and women are equally involved.

MARGARET: It could be anyone if the Spirit moves them?

ELAINE: Certainly anyone of the eldership, often called the 'oversight', but I am not even sure if it is confined to them.

I think anyone in the assembly. The elders are there to maintain good conduct and make sure that this is credal worship.
They may stop the proceedings if what is being said is not
in conformity with doctrine. Not that I have ever been in a
church where that has happened.

MARGARET: Every church that thinks it has abolished the
ordained ministry ends up by reinventing it. The fact that
those elders are authorized, any of them, to be the person who
steps forward or who re-establishes orthodoxy – that is its own
form of ordination.

ELAINE: I think it is. And nobody would quibble with the
fact that authorization of the process is vital, rather than
chaos, or being open to heresy. Even the house churches,
which are the most anarchic (if you like) Protestant groups,
have very heavy authorization patterns, very heavy leadership
patterns. But again that wouldn't be defined by the Eucharist.
It would be defined by just about everything else.

In the evangelical tradition the priest is the president, the
facilitator who reminds the church what we are doing. We see
the coming of Christ as the end of priesthood. Christ is the
great high priest, according to those wonderful passages in
the letter to the Hebrew Christians, and priestliness is an Old
Testament rather than a New Testament concept.

We also talk about the priesthood of all believers, which
was a central doctrine in the Protestant Reformation, and it
means that all the people of God are involved in making
Christ's sacrifice available. That is why in most Protestant
churches you don't need an ordained person to administer the
sacraments.

Having said all that, now that I have been so involved in the
women's ordination issue, I understand, in a way I didn't before,

what those who argue for a particular function called the priest-hood are talking about. For them, it is different from the broader sense of ministry, which is more all-embracing so it doesn't really matter whether you are male or female in the same way.

It has taken me a long time to understand how important the idea of priesthood is to those who hold it. When I left university and decided to stay within the Church of England I couldn't care whether women were priests or not because I couldn't care whether men were priests or not: I found it very hard to work up any enthusiasm on the issue. But when I recognized that whatever they thought the role was, women felt a very strong calling to it, then I became involved more for their sakes.

That is where I have been since, rather than having any deep conviction about the priesthood itself. I don't feel antag-onistic against it. I am quite happy for it to be there. But nor would I want to spend a lot of time defending it.

MARGARET: In contrast to you, I have quite a strong theolo-gy of priesthood. Of course, it has been said that if you have a strong Catholic theology of priesthood then you realize that there are theological objections to women priests. For me it does the opposite. It is because I have a strong theology of priesthood that I care so desperately about it. For women to be excluded from something that is theologically important is much worse than for them to be excluded from something that doesn't much matter.

ELAINE: Let me hear what is strong about your view of the priesthood.

MARGARET: I fully recognize that we don't have priests in the Old Testament sense any more. That entire Old Testament priesthood was replaced in Christ by the one high priest. I take that on board completely.

I also take on board completely the priesthood of all believers. There is only one priest, and we are all priestly. I acknowledge both of those positions. But I think you can have an intermediate position between those two, which doesn't contradict either of them. That is where we might begin to differ.

The priesthood, in this intermediate sense, is an expression of Christ's unique priesthood, and at the same time a focusing of the Christian people's diffuse priesthood. I see the priest as a token that sufficient conditions are present – for the group gathered here together, at this time, in this place – to celebrate Christ's sacrificial act, which is also the act of the whole church, in which we are one bread, one body.

It is not good enough to say any group of people, however small, who call themselves Christians, can celebrate that act in whatever circumstances they choose. You can get some pretty weird ideas among people who call themselves Christians. So there is a need for a church discipline to say, 'This is it. This is the Eucharist. This is an act that the whole church recognizes.'

Otherwise you could get endless splittings and fragmentations: different rites, invented rites, different theologies, variant beliefs. And everyone would be making up their own mind about which Eucharists are genuine and which aren't. So the person we call a priest is a channel through which the church guarantees that the priesthood of Christ, and the priesthood of all the believers, is operating.

At a Eucharist it is indeed the entire community that acts in a priestly way. But they do so when there is one authorized representative there, and then everyone celebrates with him. In post Vatican II theology we were suddenly taught not to talk about the priest celebrating, but the community celebrating and the priest presiding. We took on a Reformation insight which we ought to have taken on a lot earlier. I don't think it was ever denied, but it was certainly obscured.

So when I talk of having a strong theology of priesthood, I mean that I feel quite strongly that the Eucharist should not be celebrated in the absence of an ordained priest. And having someone called a priest gives me a sense of being drawn into it as a priestly act. If we didn't have a focal priest, but we all tried to remember that we were priests, I am not sure if we would have the same awareness of it being a priestly act.

But what I would like to ask you about is the differences in your church over altars or tables. That is a very visible sign of different theologies. The real Protestant thing has been to have a wooden table that reminds you of the Last Supper, and to reject the stone altar of sacrifice.

ELAINE: A central table rather than a fixed altar at the end of the church, which is only visible to the priest or the person celebrating. The central table allows the celebrant to face the people or the people to sit around it. It represents the body in action, in worship, in community. And the feast is the feast of the church.

Central and fairly unornate; although having said that I have seen central tables which have been full of symbols and dressings and equipment. People have different styles of how they treat the table.

Of course, in many Anglican churches the tradition is to have a fixed altar at the end of the sanctuary, rather than a central table. But even there the tendency over the last ten years has been for the priest to find a way of standing behind the altar. In fact, there have been rows about it. In one cathedral, where the incoming dean decided that communion would be celebrated around a central table rather than the high altar at the end, it was welcomed by the congregation, but offended some of the canons.

MARGARET: Was that an issue of wood over stone?

ELAINE: I think it was an issue of a new dean coming in and making his own decisions!

MARGARET: The Catholic position would be that the Eucharist is the Last Supper but it is also Calvary. Therefore, you can have either a wooden table with people around it to remind you that this is the Last Supper, or you can have a stone altar that is approached by steps to remind you that this is a sacrifice. And in fact even our most modern churches tend to go for the stone slab.

I thought about this a few years ago when I was at Worth Abbey in Holy Week. Have you ever been to Worth? The church is really a wonderful piece of architecture – modern and round. They had the church open late at night for silent prayer, and on Good Friday night the church was totally dark, with a single spot on the central altar, which was completely stripped. It was really dramatic to see that slab of bare, white stone lit up in the surrounding blackness.

And I thought how powerful this is. It is powerful because it evokes sacrifice, and there is the stone. You are reminded of the Old Testament echoes, now replaced in Christ, but still there is blood spilt. It is pretty strong stuff. So it seems to me a pity if a powerful side can't be recognized, if it is made too clean.

ELAINE: I don't think that is missing in Anglicanism, and certainly the cross will be the predominant image in the communion service. It is only because of the cross, the sacrifice, otherwise there is nothing to celebrate. But what are we celebrating? Certainly the atonement rather than the sacrifice. This is bound to give the Eucharist a slightly different nuance. We are celebrating the effects of what Christ did rather than re-live the barbaric and horrendous details.

Sometimes it's very appropriate to remember those details in awe, because that barbarism was real and it has so many implications. We certainly think about it solemnly, and it's very much part of the Eucharist. But we don't dwell on that too much (except on Good Friday) and we don't re-enact it in communion. The greater focus is on the body now rather than the body then, the living body rather than the dead Saviour; the raised body of Christ, and the body that Christ has left behind on earth.

Maybe this is simply a different nuance, which opens up the sense of where we go from here. It does not seem necessary to dwell only on something that is completed, finished and doesn't need to be done again.

MARGARET: I am perfectly happy with the idea of all those aspects being present in one Eucharist: the Resurrection, and the body of Christ in the church today, as well as the Last Supper and the Crucifixion. But I think sometimes it is good to stress one and sometimes another.

ELAINE: And that is almost the position I have come to. We are horribly in agreement again!

Years ago, as a child, I knew very little about Catholicism, but my mother was High Anglican. The difference between her Anglo-Catholicism and Roman Catholicism was supposed to be the Eucharist. Our headmaster, who belonged to the church my mother had been brought up in, used to explain it in class, but for the life of me I couldn't see that much difference.

MARGARET: Between what and what?

ELAINE: Between the High Anglican position and the Catholic position. Transubstantiation was always given as the doctrine that the High Anglicans didn't believe in, but when you asked, 'What do you believe in? What are you doing?' it sounded just the same.

I remember our headmaster offering a refutation of transubstantiation. He pointed out that if chemical tests were carried out on what was in the chalice it wouldn't turn out to be blood, but only wine. And I would think, 'I am sure that Catholics are aware of that. Surely they don't believe that if you analyse the chemical elements this would be blood?'

MARGARET: Of course we don't, that is the point of the doctrine of transubstantiation. People don't talk much about transubstantiation nowadays and it is not thought a very useful way of explaining the Eucharist, but the one time it does become useful is when people talk about chemical experiments. What transubstantiation says is precisely that you will then get the answer, 'This is wine,' because the chemical qualities, which we call the 'accidents', are unchanged. The sense in which it becomes Christ's blood, what we call a change of 'substance', is something quite different from anything relevant to scientific testing.

ELAINE: It has been a long process, stripping away a lot of strange myths about what Catholics believe, which hung around when I was a child. A lot of it was confused and got mixed up with folklore and superstition. And now I rarely hear this kind of discussion taking place at all. Certainly not in England.

MARGARET: While Catholics don't talk so much about transubstantiation these days, we would still want to stress that the Eucharist is more than just symbolic, more than just a memorial – though it is that as well. Even in the words of Jesus himself, you can find both the symbolic dimension and a dimension that goes beyond that and becomes itself a reality. The memorial is there in 'Do this in memory of me.' But he also says, 'This is my body.'

When we had the Tridentine Mass, you just could not see how it was a memorial of the Last Supper. It seemed to have moved away from that completely. But on the other hand, if you overemphasize 'Do this in memory of me' to mean 'I am only doing it as a reminder', then it does not do justice to the fullness of the Eucharist. Jesus was not saying, 'Let's have a little think about things and while we are thinking let's hold this bread.' He is saying something more powerful than that. It is commemoration in the strong sense.

ELAINE: When Anglicans are offered the elements we are told, this is 'the body of Our Lord Jesus Christ which he gave for you, and his blood which he shed for you', and we respond with 'Amen'. When we do that we are not simply remembering the Last Supper. We are receiving the body and blood of Christ, but clearly not the literal body and blood, because even when Christ said, 'This is my body,' he was standing there and that was his body. So we feel we must receive it in the way that he intended, which is in some deep metaphorical or what some call a sacramental sense.

MARGARET: Yes, I'm happy with all that. This comes back to blood and sacrifice. The Catholic position has always been that there is only one event. But through the mystery of eternity one can tap into that event through a different moment in time. It wasn't done once at the Last Supper and then repeated at Calvary; it was the same sacrifice, and it is the same again at every Mass.

Instead of just those few women at the foot of the cross being so privileged to be there, present while Christ was dying to thank him for his sacrifice in the very presence of it, to say 'Yes' to it, to ask for graces, to make whatever prayers one might be moved to make at such a moment – instead of just those women being privileged, we all have access to the same closeness. Not just through imagination and memory, but in a sense we can be as really present to it as they were who were historically there. There's a new way into understanding the real presence.

ELAINE: I would like to go away and think more about that. I have never thought of the real presence in those terms. I have always thought that the real presence must mean Christ with us now rather than us with Christ then. That is very interesting.

MARGARET: I think that idea is important also with the Last Supper. It's not as though the people who were at the original event had the best deal and all we can do is watch a video. The Mass makes us present at the Last Supper, as the mystery of God breaks through the limits of time. So it's a mistake to place too much emphasis on who was really there: was it just the twelve? Was Jesus' mother there? Were the other women there? There is not that kind of hierarchy over historical presence. We are all really there.

ELAINE: Yes, I have certainly no problem with that. I have had the experience of being one with the church through the ages, and one with the disciples who leaned on Christ's breast, in a very profound way during the Eucharist. One can only call it a mystical experience of the church in union.

MARGARET: That same principle of the real presence despite the barriers of time and space has made the Eucharist easier for me now that Peter is dead, in that it has given it a new meaning for me, that we can have a meal together again. The meal is the heavenly banquet in which he is already sharing in a better way, a fuller way, than ever before, but in which he is united to me through the Eucharist.

These days, when I receive communion, instead of sitting there feeling cross about women's ordination, I am more likely to feel mystically united with Peter through Christ. Jesus and Peter and I all sit down and eat together. That is the same principle as being united with those at the first event.

But the reason why I feel so cross is because the issue of the priesthood links up very much with the icon of Christ. For me this is the most painful aspect of the opposition to women's ordination. In the days not so long ago when women's priesthood was just something that no one had thought of, then the ban wasn't nearly so offensive. It was just something that wasn't done, but there was no great theological weight attached to it.

ELAINE: That is a very important point. When it was merely tradition, and part of patriarchy as it existed everywhere else in society, then you just shrugged your shoulders and recognized it as the ball game. It was the convention.

But then, when, in order to resist change, it became reinforced by theology and by new ways of describing God and affirming maleness, it became, as you say...

MARGARET: ... a terribly important issue.

In past centuries the arguments against women priests, when they were given at all, were arguments that would not be accepted nowadays. They were evidently demeaning to women. What I feel so strongly about is that the theological arguments today against women's ordination are not traditional arguments, they are new ones. That is why I was so pleased when George Carey made his controversial statement about heresy, which he afterwards retracted, that it was 'a most serious heresy' to say only a male could represent Christ at the altar.

Once you say, 'The priest is the icon of Christ,' and then you add, 'and women can't be icons of Christ,' it's awful. So awful. I mean I can't believe how anyone could dare say it.

I went to four ordinations of women priests in the Church of England – Bristol, Oxford, London and Coventry. They were very emotional events, and another emotional event was the first Eucharist celebrated by the moderator of the Movement for the Ordination of Women, Cathy Milford. It was a great beano in the course of MOW's final conference.

I think the reason why people cared so much, and why they were so moved, was because this was the open, communal affirmation at last, that women are icons of Christ in the same way that men are. They don't have a lesser likeness to Christ. It is fundamental.

ELAINE: The whole issue of icon as representation has been terribly misused. It seems 'icon' has been taken to include all the particularities about gender but to ignore all the other particularities, such as Christ's Jewishness, or the fact that he was in the first century, or that he was a carpenter. The more all these other particularities were cut away, and one specific feature remained, then the more painful it became and the more damaging for women.

MARGARET: Exactly. And people are still saying that a woman can't represent Christ in this central priestly act of our salvation, in what is the whole point of the incarnation, the way in which he saves us. That is where we do not have the likeness. And the more they make that point, the worse it becomes.

ELAINE: Yes, that is an extraordinary assertion. It takes one's breath away.

MARGARET: And that is why I say having a strong view of the priesthood and of the Eucharist as a priestly act makes me care more about women's priesthood than I would otherwise.

ELAINE: I haven't shared that strong sense of the priesthood. Nevertheless, when I have heard the arguments as to why it should be restricted to men, I have found them so very inadequate. And when we see the poverty of the arguments underlying such a dogmatic position the issue becomes painful and wrong and damaging and misogynist. It belittles Christ's atonement, ignores the thrust of the scriptures and de-radicalizes the faith. It has made me so angry that I have wanted to go for it with everything I've got.

One of the most striking moments for me came when I was at a debate in one of the London deaneries on why women couldn't be priests, in the build-up to the General Synod decision. Some women deacons were sitting in the front row. They had been already affirmed by the church in their calling to the diaconate and were trained alongside the men. I looked at one of them who sat patiently and noticed that she was clenching her hands, and her knuckles were quite white. In spite of her external demeanour she obviously was finding it hard to cope with the tone and attitudes displayed by the men. It was an all-clergy gathering, and in that deanery the male clergy present were overwhelmingly opposed to the ordination of women.

When I saw this particular woman, externally calm but with these white knuckles and her face drained of colour, I thought, 'Oh boy, whatever must it be like to be in that position: hearing words dismissing both your calling and your identity?' I felt both compassion and anger at the same time. I had an overwhelming desire to punch one of the most insensitive men!

The whole debate was grim. I spoke, coherently I thought, for women's ordination, but found myself quite patronized. There were heated opinions and some did everything they could to undermine what I was saying, often more by attitude than argument. I didn't care. I was happy to do it because my own calling was somewhere else and therefore it was far easier for me.

MARGARET: How were you present at a deanery meeting?

ELAINE: I was invited to speak. None of the women deacons wanted to do it. And I understood why afterwards. The pain was just too much. It was a sobering experience for me, and a turning point to see such anxiety and pain. I was surprised that Christian men could speak like that. The level of rudeness would not have been tolerated in any other professional setting I had been in. How could they do it?

MARGARET: That's right. It's the most insulting thing they could possibly say, no matter how it's wrapped up with 'women are different and wonderful and beautiful and we so esteem them'. Because they are also saying, 'The nature of their difference is that they cannot represent Christ, but we can.' You couldn't say anything more insulting.

ELAINE: Having a strong view of the priesthood does make the issue much more painful than it is for people in the Protestant Church who don't. In most Protestant churches women aren't usually excluded from office, even, for example, from the office of evangelist. Yet men still predominate because evangelism is simply more associated with a 'male' style: loud voice, commanding presence, authoritative pronouncements and so on.

It's the same in pastoral ministry. Women are not excluded, but there are far more men around. The arguments are that women often have divided priorities, especially if they are mothers. So it is unwise to encourage them to be pastors of a church when they are bringing up small children, where the same is not true of fathers. The end result might be similar, but the reasons are less difficult to overcome. And we can understand some of these reservations and they can be discussed.

But if you say ontologically, in the nature of humanity, women may not represent Christ, then you are saying something very, very different.

MARGARET: And it shouldn't happen because the theology is there and has been stressed ever since the Reformation – that all believers belong to the priesthood, and therefore priestliness is in us all. What is essential to priestliness is to offer Christ's sacrifice, to join with him in saying: 'This was an awful sacrifice, but I offer it, and I offer myself with it,' and we have always been taught not only that we can make that prayer, but that we must make it. When we say 'Amen' to the blood of Christ, we are actually joining in the sacrificial offering of Christ.

ELAINE: In the Protestant tradition we don't join in the sacrificial offering: we can't do anything other than receive it. We are not part of the offering, although in a sense we offer ourselves through Christ, and Christ accepts our offering to him. But the sacrifice is his alone, and our sacrifices are of a different nature.

MARGARET: But if we say 'Yes' to his sacrifice, then that is to offer it, is it not?

ELAINE: What are we doing? Are we or Christ offering the sacrifice? We are making it available to all who come and receive it. And we are receiving it with gratitude.

MARGARET: Think, for example, of his mother Mary, who in some sense had to say 'Yes' to God's will, and did say in effect, 'Yes, you can take my son from me.' She offered him.

ELAINE: I'm not sure that Mary offered Christ as sacrifice. Didn't she just recognize what obedience was going to mean in his life and hers? The issue is whether or not we are part of the redemptive process, or whether we receive the redemption. That is the difference of emphasis.

MARGARET: This links up with whether you use the word 'priest', doesn't it?

ELAINE: Yes, that's right, it does, completely. So why is it, then, that there is such opposition within the Catholic Church to women being priests? Is it just tradition? Is it fear? In my hearing it is always couched against something called feminism: 'The women who want to do this are feminists, and most women don't want this.'

MARGARET: You say there is such opposition within the Catholic Church, but if you take the hierarchy out of it, there isn't the opposition. I know very few Catholics who are opposed to the ordination of women.

ELAINE: Well, I don't know many, either. But that's probably because my Catholic friends are like you and me, and that is why we are friends!

MARGARET: Yes, one never knows how distorted one's view is because of that factor.

ELAINE: But it is true that, among the Catholics I teach at the Institute, for example, I haven't yet found anyone who was prepared to stand up and say, 'I don't think women should be priests.'

MARGARET: Yes, and I think you will find a lot of people who are very strongly in favour, as I am. I think also you will find a lot of people who don't feel particularly strongly about it, because it is not on our agenda, it is not going to happen. Anyone who campaigns for it within the Catholic Church at the moment is wasting their time.

But you can argue historically and say you need a lot of people to waste their time for an awfully long period before things begin to change, so in a sense your time is never wasted.

I have never so far joined the group called CWO (Catholic Women's Ordination), which is the Catholic branch of MOW, because when it was started I thought it was strategically a mistake and likely to call out a counter-reaction from Rome. Now that has happened with this so-called infallible teaching. So maybe I should join CWO now, because the damage has been done.

But you ask, 'Why is there this opposition?' and there certainly is enormously strong opposition from Rome. Some of it is personal to the Pope, and I think that has a lot to do with the fact that he lost his mother when he was a small child. So the mother figure is very important to him, and he cares that a woman should be a woman and not just an imitation man. Mary the mother of Jesus is very important to him, and women's vocation to motherhood is very important to him. I think he feels that is under threat.

That is one strand. Another is the result of having lived all his life under Communism, where preserving the faith unquestioningly, as it has come to you, was a badge of loyalty. So I think he has personal reasons for his strong stance.

But for the rest, the Roman Curia and so on, I think it is much more to do with control, and preserving what used to be called class-interest. It would be a complete revolution in practical terms. Allow one little hole in the dam and everything would fall apart. It would be quite dramatic. So the simplest thing to do is hold tight where you are.

ELAINE: That is very sad.

Eight

BEING LAY

MARGARET: Considering both you and I are lay-people and yet we have these extraordinarily strong views on the access of women to the priesthood, it would be interesting to talk about why we haven't chosen that path for ourselves. Not that I, as a Catholic, can choose for myself. But why haven't you sought ordination?

ELAINE: When I was a young woman, thinking about what I might do in the future, it never crossed my mind. I don't think I was a very 'churchy' kind of person. Those women who were went into orders of some kind, became nuns. There were also deaconesses, but that kind of role looked rather unattractive to a young woman. The general impression was of middle-aged, greyish kinds of ladies on the edges of visibility who seemed to have to fuss around the vicar and make sure he had plenty of tea at parish meetings. It wasn't exactly the dynamic kind of career young academic women of my generation were itching to develop.

MARGARET: You may get some offended letters from deaconesses.

ELAINE: Well, obviously my impressions were not reliable, and what deaconesses did in reality was a long way from what it seemed like to a 17-year-old. But the impressions were enough for me never to consider the option.

MARGARET: Deaconesses were only just starting up, weren't they?

ELAINE: Yes. And it is evident even now that there was not much status or leadership attached to the role. Deaconesses were not ordained clergy. Some people felt they were somewhere in between social workers, vicars' wives and housekeepers; their role was not fully defined. But, actually, these were phenomenal women; so dedicated to the calling that they were prepared to put up with the anomalies to serve the church, which I clearly wasn't. I had to learn a bit more about servanthood later. It wasn't only deaconesses but clergy themselves who failed to attract me to any church-focused employment. Most clergymen I met were on the whole doddery, woolly men quite out of touch with normality who didn't think very clearly. Why would anyone want to be like that? Later on, when it became evident that things were going to change in the church, I had already felt God was calling me in an academic direction. Then I married, had children, and stayed at home with them. By the time I was in my early thirties it was evident that sooner or later women were going to be ordained, at least into the diaconate. I remember a flurry of excitement among women who had known all along their calling was to ordination. Somebody suggested that mine might be, but I still couldn't enter a profession where there were inbuilt structures to make sure that women stayed at a certain level. It felt like a personal compromise, buying into a structure which was fundamentally sexist and where women always would be seen as second best. It was probably pride, too.

MARGARET: What about since women have been admitted to the priesthood? After all, there are a number of very talented women, like Angela Tilby, who have only come into this at the last minute after the doors were opened. Although even now the doors are not open to women in the way that they are to men, because of the discrimination in the Act of Synod.

ELAINE: That's right. I think since the full measure was passed I have felt I was too old to begin the whole process, even if I had felt any kind of calling.

MARGARET: Too old? But so many women have been ordained. Una Kroll, you know. I was at her ordination.

ELAINE: But she was already ordained deacon before she became a priest and had been working within the church for quite a while.

MARGARET: But, Elaine, you don't need it, because you are Elaine Storkey!

ELAINE: I'm also the sort of person who feels she can work within and between churches, communities, denominations and the rest of society. I value the flexibility of that very much.

But I suppose there is also something deep inside me that would love to nurture a congregation. I realized that in one parish, where I was aware how badly it was being done. I thought: these people need to be loved, not just lectured to; to be nurtured and enabled to grow. It did cross my mind that I'd love to do it, but I went out of the door and realized I'd got a different kind of calling.

If I'd been born in another decade it might have been different. In the Church of England there is so much scope now for women clergy. The clergy role is a combination of so many things that women are good at: nurturing, loving, organizing, managing people, preaching, networking with people, encouraging, counselling, setting examples. There's also a strong teaching ministry there which is challenging intellectually.

I've always felt called to be a communicator and to teach in the broadest way. Recently I've felt called to nurture people more – not just in terms of family, but more widely than that. I don't know what more a calling to the priesthood would mean other than recognizing that it fits a deep sense that God is with you in these areas, and you're equipped for them. Yet I've talked to women who've known ever since they could remember that they were called to the priesthood.

MARGARET: Really?

ELAINE: Oh yes. One friend told me she had asked God about it since she was a small child.

MARGARET: I'm reminded of the way St Bernard talks about the priest as mother, because the bit that appeals to you is so much that maternal role. The nurturing and seeing people grow is so precious and special. No wonder male priests aren't always good at it, although, of course, many of them are absolutely wonderful at it.

Then there is another side which is a disadvantage, because if you're going to do that mothering bit properly and nurture people, you can't be a national figure or globetrotter, disappearing and putting the media and the wider world first. That's the tension, isn't it?

ELAINE: Yes, it is. It is. And that's the tension I actually face both with my family and at the Institute. I would like to spend more time with my staff there. It bothers me when I see colleagues struggle with various personal issues that I feel I could help them with. They are mature Christians, but it helps to share things. Yet the time I have been able to give to helping staff in this way is limited.

MARGARET: Can you maybe say a little bit more about the positive sides of being lay? Because it's not just a negative thing.

ELAINE: No, for me being a laywoman has been incredibly positive. I have felt I've had a more mediating role as a woman, which I wouldn't have had as a man. Also, I think I've helped the cause for women priests by not being ordained, and by therefore not being any threat to ordained men. For a decade I probably got more invitations to speak at different churches, diocesan conferences and synods because I was lay than I would ever have received had I been ordained. Women's ordination was far too sensitive and divisive an issue.

There was an issue, too, about not wanting to be divisive about churchmanship: ordained people come into certain kinds of camps: evangelical, Catholic, liberal, charismatic and numerous variations of those. So if a bishop wanted to be inclusive of the varieties of theological positions in the diocese a sensible thing was to ask someone who would be acceptable to all groups. Ordained women weren't.

I think it was because I was known more as a sociologist than as a theologian (although I lecture in theology at present) that I have been able to go where other women have not been asked. The good thing is that it helps men who have never sat under women's ministry, because they can make their own evaluation of my Bible studies or lectures without pressure. Sometimes the audiences have included clergy who would have had an ordained woman in their parish only over their dead bodies. Yet they have usually received what I have said with respect, and I hope I have challenged their own preconceptions even a little. I am sure that has to be positive, and that's one of the tasks as a layperson I've had marvellous freedom for.

Of course, we are moving into a decade where ordained women can do that too, and there won't be the same problems. Yet even recently a bishop friend mentioned to me that he wanted to invite as keynote speaker an ordained woman who now held a position of some authority in the church. But among some of his clergy there were so many objections to a woman who had moved so far and so fast that he did not want to trigger off letters of complaint.

MARGARET: Really?

ELAINE: Oh yes. If you have 'two integrities' then that means to a lot of people that you are entitled to refuse to have women in these roles.

MARGARET: Yes, I can quite see that. I thought the 'two integrities' would work out even worse than it has done. People were so naive about the negative consequences. I always assumed it could mean that for anything that happened at a deanery or diocesan or national level you'd only need one person to say, 'I'm of the other integrity and I veto a woman because she doesn't speak for me.'

ELAINE: That's precisely it, you see. Somehow, you are accused of not following 'two integrities', only one, by trying to push an ordained woman in higher leadership! But the questions are not raised when I speak, because I'm not ordained and there's no threat. And in that sense it's been good being no threat, and yet being able to minister and affirm women who are ministering.

I've never had any woman come up to me and say, 'I resent the fact that you're doing this and I'm not able to.' They have usually come up and said, 'Thanks so much for being here: things are moving slowly, but they're moving.' And then they've told me some sad stories and some very happy stories about working in their own parishes.

MARGARET: I have heard just a tiny bit about the difficulties of this 'two integrities' business, but I don't really rub up against examples. How painful and ironic that you talk about women not resenting the fact that you can do things that they can't do, precisely because they are ordained. It's a complete reversal of what things were before.

ELAINE: But they know that it is all changing and ordination is their calling. Now there are only a few things that women can't do. Of course, that doesn't mean that women in ordained leadership are very numerous.

MARGARET: My feelings and responses are very, very similar to yours, and everything you have said makes complete sense, and yet I come at it from a totally different church background so the incidentals are different.

For me as an adolescent the dominant myth was if you have a 'vocation' then that means if you're a man you become a priest and if you're a woman you become a nun. And I didn't want to become a nun. Like you with the deaconesses, I didn't find that an inspiring role model, or even a role model that I thought was an example of godliness. To have the Christian gospel symbolized by dressing yourself in black and hiding your hair and wearing sensible lace-up shoes – well, it's worse than irrelevant to the gospel, it's pedalling fast in the opposite direction. That was changing, but it was only changing very slowly. So I didn't want to be a nun. From that point of view I had to be a layperson.

I think there's also a very individualist streak in my personality. We talk a lot in the Catholic Church about the importance of collaborative ministry, and this is something women are generally very strong on. I have to confess that I don't think I am. I'm much more someone who wants to take a different line, disagree with the consensus and do things myself because I can't quite trust anyone else to do it my way. All those kinds of faults that you see in a male clergy I see in myself. So that personality trait fitted me to plough my own furrow in a way, and not move into any ready-made Christian way of life.

Of course, the priesthood wasn't open to me. I only began to think about the issue of women priests in my late twenties really, as late as that, and I was one of the first Catholics to do so. I think that's the problem in so many other countries of the world where you don't find support for it among Catholics: people haven't thought of it. And I didn't think of it.

But then there's more to it than not wanting to be a priest, and not wanting to be a nun, and being individualist. There's another strand, too. When I read theology at Oxford, laypeople were just beginning to do that, people who were not in training for the Anglican ministry. I wasn't one of the very first, but it was within a few years. That change happened quite quickly, and when it did change a lot of women wanted to read theology. I wanted to read theology because I loved it and not because this was something I needed to do as a qualification for something else. It felt very good to do it out of pure love for the subject, without using it as a means to something else.

Then there is pastoral work. That was a desire that was very definitely awakened in me in my period of living in Rome. I went to the Gregorian because I wanted to continue with theology, and that was the best of the universities there for that, and it just happened, you know, with almost everyone there a priest or a religious. I was studying alongside these people who were all coming from pastoral situations and going back into pastoral situations, sometimes very dangerous ones in very remote parts of the world. By the time I left that had awakened in me a desire to do the same in my own lay way.

Again, it would have seemed a terrible cop-out – and of course it wasn't open to me anyway, because by this time I was married with two children, and the third on the way by the time we'd left Rome – to say, 'I would like to do pastoral work so I'll become a nun.' But it was more than just that it wasn't possible, you know: there was a very important ideological point that you don't have to be a priest or a nun to do this.

And that became increasingly important in the decade of the eighties. (We came back in 1981.) It was really a crusade to show how every Christian person could live out the apostolate fully. If there was the slightest hint that you had to become a priest or a nun in order to do it better or do it at all, it would have undermined really the whole Christian enterprise...

ELAINE: Completely, yes.

MARGARET: ...which is to everyone. 'Go therefore and make disciples of all nations, baptising them ...' (Matthew 28:19). In Catholic theology, by the way, baptism can be administered by laity.

ELAINE: Oh, right?

MARGARET: And a friend of mine in Kenya was in fact baptized by someone who was not only a layman but a leper, because as a baby his life was in danger. Which is a beautiful thing.

ELAINE: Yes, wonderful.

MARGARET: And that's not 'redone properly' by the clergy – it is valid baptism and can't be repeated.

So at that stage I felt very strongly that my vocation was to be a layperson, and through my own initiative to push open doors and make the way for other laypeople to walk through them, for it wasn't as though I was the only person struggling to do this.

One of the areas that was very important to me then was Ignatian spirituality, which had been crucial in my own spiritual development, just before Rome and during Rome. I very much wanted to hand that on to other people, particularly to people who were tied at home because they had small children and therefore couldn't go away in the way a priest or a religious could to a retreat house. It is harder if you struggle to do it while you're at home with little children, but the point was to make it possible. So it was a really great crusade.

Then we had, in the Catholic Church, a Synod on the laity…

ELAINE: Yes, I remember that.

MARGARET: …which I don't think yielded any fruits that I've noticed in terms of Rome recognizing the lay vocation or lay ministry, but it did provide an opportunity for laypeople to get together and talk about this among themselves. Peter and I, both of us, were very much involved in that. We ran a series of seminars in Oxford which were very successful.

After that we organized something called the Laity Consultation, which was a weekend event in Oxford, open to laypeople all over the country, and they came and stayed in people's homes. We produced a document out of that, so that was all great fun, a great sense of thrusting forward.

ELAINE: That sense of dignity and recognition for the laity, of not seeing the clergy as the norm for Christian discipleship, has been part of my mentality, too, from my earliest days as a Christian. Certainly it was there right through the university years, partly because of the IVF movement.

MARGARET: What's that?

ELAINE: The Inter-Varsity Fellowship as it was then; it's now the UCCF (Universities and Colleges Christian Fellowship). It's a nationwide fellowship of evangelical students, linked with an international group, the IFES (International Fellowship of Evangelical Students). I don't think I realized until later in life what a personal blessing this fellowship had been. It both gave me a Christian identity in a very secular context, and challenged me to integrate my biblical faith with study. Groups exist in almost all universities, and because it is interdenominational, and not a church, clergy don't really feature. Students themselves lead the Bible studies and prayer meetings. It has always been a lay movement, and reinforced the sense of empowerment and all the positive qualities of being lay.

It also helped to reintegrate fragmentations within Protestantism. These two central ideas, that there was no real

clergy/lay divide, and that denominations are not huge barriers that you can never climb over, have been important to me,
ever since my UCCF days.

Chaplains have always found the groups a bit trying, especially because they quickly find they have no more authority
there than the students. Their theology is often examined and
frequently challenged, rather than taken on board simply
because they are ordained. Some chaplains were very good at
listening and encouraging, and their pastoral help was usually
appreciated.

I must admit that we were student upstarts. As an older person, I see it slightly differently, but then it was all to do with
having confidence in one's faith and power in believing and I
don't think that has ever gone. As young lay students we were
invited to work out our faith, struggle with scriptural teaching,
look at church history, issues in relationships, big questions
about estrangement from God, redemption, Christology, Trinity.
It wasn't a formal theological educational programme, just
something that took place week by week in meetings where
books of the Bible were worked through systematically. We
sang, prayed and then sat down to these fine expository talks.

Looking back, it was an incredibly rich upbringing, even
with its limitations. So it's interesting that within different
church traditions we've travelled a similarly liberating lay
route.

Alan's first job outside academia was with a lay study project; the Shaftesbury Project was essentially a lay organization
within the church.

MARGARET: Alan's not ordained, is he?

ELAINE: No. He and I feel exactly the same on this. Again, it
has been suggested many times that he should be ordained,

but he's never yet felt this to be right. He's called to be a layperson.

MARGARET: Do you know Martin Conway, who was President of Selly Oak Colleges? I talked to him about this, because he's a layperson.

ELAINE: Oh, I didn't realize that he was lay, I just assumed he was ordained.

MARGARET: Well, there you are, you see: isn't it awful that we're so conditioned that one assumes that? No, he's lay, and I think several times in his life he has found it difficult to get jobs because of that. Before he got the Selly Oak one I talked to him about the theology of the laity, and he said that someone once said to him, 'Isn't it time you turned your collar round, old boy?' And his response was, 'What do you think the whole thing's about, anyway?'

This is it. You can't read the Gospels about not seeking positions of authority, and not walking around in long robes, and not seeking special titles, and the last will be first – you can't do that and say, 'I'm going to become clerical because it will make life easy for me and open doors.'

ELAINE: Oh quite, I agree. That was always my fear, that ordination could mean that women would just fall in line behind the ordained men, rather than realizing there is a whole other dimension to leadership.

MARGARET: Well, that's what a lot of people say. But in my experience it's not at all the case.

ELAINE: No, it isn't in mine, except in one or two instances. One experience at Synod did bother me. For years we've had fringe meetings about issues of particular concern to women. During the run-up to the ordination debate, many of them were inevitably about ordination, but there have always been other key concerns.

At one meeting after the ordination measure had been passed we had a meeting on violence to women. The paper contained very disturbing figures and was a pointed challenge to the churches. I was one of the speakers and the meeting was well attended, but when I looked around I noticed there wasn't a single woman priest there. This was very unusual, because their attendance had always been very strong before. When I enquired afterwards where they were, I was told that our meeting had clashed with a meeting about clergy pensions, and they had all gone to that.

It was quite a sore point for some of us in the fringe meeting!

MARGARET: Like you, I have chosen this lay way of life, but I feel the element of tug the other way. Or I shouldn't say 'tug' exactly – that's too strong. The hierarchy of the Catholic Church at the moment is so unattractive that it puts off a lot of idealistic young men as well as the women. There is a sense in which people want to withdraw their labour from such a corrupt system and not put themselves in a position where they would have to be discreet in their criticisms.

But all the same, my position has softened from a complete certainty that I'm called to be a layperson. I could envisage being a priest now, and that's because there are so many things that I do which belong also to the priestly way of life. When you talk about nurturing a congregation, I think possibly that is the most important one. It's the sense of actually being the person with authority – not to do what you like with a congregation in the sense of bossing it around, but just to have that freedom not to be hindered in pushing forward radical plans.

ELAINE: Women have either had to stand behind the man and try to do it all through him, or else some have stood on their own, shouting at a distance in a discontented way –

MARGARET: Exactly.

ELAINE: – or some have whipped up support among the laity and formed little factions which produce contentions for power. And all of those are so very unsatisfactory.

MARGARET: Exactly. I've lived through all of those, I've tried them all, and they're all unsatisfactory in different ways.

ELAINE: So it's actually, as you say, a matter of having the agreed authority to do it in an uncomplicated, unapologetic way, where you don't have to justify yourself or feel defensive.

MARGARET: Sometimes that is the way you work. There's an interesting example that comes to my mind of a Catholic diocese which is really plugging base communities, and the bishop is pushing it, but the pastoral letters that say 'this is our pastoral plan' are written by his pastoral team – a majority of whom are women. It's the vicar's wife syndrome, if you like. The ideas are not his ideas, but he can see it is a good thing to do. And without him being on that side and saying, 'You tell me what to say and I'll say it,' it couldn't happen.

And, of course, that happens the entire time, doesn't it, with politicians and with senior clerics like the Archbishop of

Canterbury? I mean, any idea that they write all their own
speeches is absurd: they take the credit for ideas developed by
other people. But it's more difficult with the issue of women
in parishes, because then it's not a matter of distributing
responsibilities, it's a function of women being banned from
operating on an equal basis with men.

Nine

THE OLD TESTAMENT

MARGARET: How can a Christian feminist cope with the male bias of the scriptures, particularly in passages that are deeply offensive to women? To what extent are we bound by the Bible? How would an evangelical feminist and a Catholic feminist differ in their approach to the scriptures? And what are some of the most illuminating insights of feminism in reading the Bible?

ELAINE: I have been looking forward to this, possibly because I have not talked about the Bible with many Catholics at all. I'm interested in exploring that alone, even apart from all the implications that it has for feminism. Evangelicals have always wanted to be people of the Book, seeing their own authority stemming from biblical authority, and they have always been suspicious of Christians who do not seem to have a biblical backing for their position. I'm not at all sure that evangelicals have always got biblical authority right, but I am still interested to explore what our differences are in approaching scriptures.

So what are you going to tell me?

MARGARET: Starting with that question, before going into the question of particular passages that are difficult, I think there is a difference in the Catholic approach to the Bible. We would regard the Bible as normative, but we would see it as the Book of the people of God, that emerges out of the history of the people.

The great Reformation controversy was between *scriptura sola* (scripture alone, the Protestant position) or scripture and tradition (the Catholic position). We would see tradition as being deeply interwoven into the production of the biblical text in the first place. Then tradition continues in the ongoing history of the people of God, and in the ongoing interpretation of the biblical text. So that the scriptures come to us through tradition.

Then the canon of the scriptures is established through the authority of the church. They did not drop down from heaven like the ten commandments written on stone on Mount Sinai. Therefore the Bible cannot be given an authority above tradition, because tradition has actually produced the Bible. The two go completely hand in hand.

And that affects the way we look at texts from scripture today. You know the phrase which I always associate with evangelicals: 'The Bible says ...' As though it was always one voice, one coherent teaching. Catholics would be suspicious of that kind of language. Though we do it ourselves in our own way, in having our favourite bits: 'Thou art Peter and upon this rock I will build my church.' But actually, I haven't heard a Catholic quote that in years.

So for Catholics it would be a matter of taking the history of the people of God as sacred – because it is the history of salvation – and the Book is the record of that salvation history. It gets its sanctity out of being the officially authorized version of that story – the canon. But it is an ongoing story, it continues today.

This is something I have noticed through the base communities of Latin America, the way they will take a passage of scripture and interpret it in terms of their own experience, their own life. They talk about text, context and pre-text – at least that is the way a scripture scholar in Brazil, Carlos Mesters, puts it. The pre-text is their own life, the text is the scripture, and the context is the community discussing it. He says: 'It is like a violin. The text is the strings, the context is the sound-box, and the pre-text is the reason for playing' (*Defenseless Flower: a new reading of the Bible*, Orbis 1989, p. 109).

So the text does not stand alone. The inspiration of the Spirit happens through the gelling together of that process. It is not just in the text as something fixed. The text becomes a living text, added to and interpreted in the ongoing history of the people of God.

ELAINE: I think actually my position is not that far away, except that the difference between us is that tradition for me has to come lower than scripture. Otherwise, what yardstick do we have to decide whether something is a biblical tradition or a non-biblical tradition? When is tradition in error? When does tradition lapse into superstition? How do we know if we are simply making it up as we go along?

And so the Protestant evangelical believes that at the end of the day scripture is always the touchstone. We can only assess all those things – and see when the tradition takes off into heresy – by going to look at the scriptures themselves. That remains my position.

But having said that I don't know whether I have ever said, 'The Bible says ...' and used that as a proof text. If I did it was a very long time ago, and I cringe the moment anybody else says it. Most evangelicals today recognize the Bible as a very complex document. In fact, it is not one book but a whole library, and as such needs careful hermeneutics in order to be understood.

God is revealed in many ways: through creation, through the church, and supremely through Christ, the incarnate Word, the Word made Flesh. But it is the scriptures which unlock those things to us. We only know Jesus as the Christ through the scriptures and as experienced within the church through the power of the Holy Spirit. Otherwise we don't know him.

Similarly, we don't really know that the 'natural order' is God's creation, except insofar as it is disclosed to us by the Holy Spirit through the scriptures. The scriptures tell us more than about the tradition, or church. They open up for us the whole of reality.

For example, we go to the world in order to understand science – but we gain our understanding within a biblical framework. There are big themes in the Bible which give us a perspective on the whole of reality: such themes as creation, human sin, redemption, the coming of the Spirit, the end times, and so on, and within that framework there are so many other biblical insights that we bring to bear on any issue. But even to say this (or anything else) is to filter the Bible through a hermeneutical framework.

In the unfolding development of God's revelation to us, we don't understand it all at once, complete. Our knowledge unfolds gradually; we see bits of it now and bits of it later. That is true of the so-called difficult texts. So they are not for me the deep problem that they are for many evangelicals.

MARGARET: It is some consolation that it is not just a matter of passages that are difficult for feminists, but of passages that are difficult for us all.

I completely agree with you about the complexity of the hermeneutic that is needed, taking the whole rather than extracting bits. The parts are judged by the whole and by a very sensitive and wise and attentive openness to the underlying spirit of it.

That would also be my defence of tradition. We have got awful bits of tradition just as we have got difficult passages of scripture. The current Pope's key to how to tell which tradition is authentic is, 'The magisterium of the church tells you.' That is, he tells you. Which won't do.

Whether it is scripture or tradition or our own lives, interpretation is always an open-ended process. It is never an infallible process, but a process of discernment in which you take the overall spirit. I think you can find a parallel to the idea of reception in reading the scriptures.

ELAINE: Most evangelicals will claim that the scriptures can't be wrong. But we can certainly get the scriptures wrong, can fail to understand where we are in the big picture, or what the Spirit is saying to the church at this point. Most of the errors come from a combination of our arrogance and our fallibility.

There is a whole debate about the inerrancy of scripture which I have never begun to understand. The very word 'inerrant' is an odd one: tapping into a theory of truth which limits it to the sum total of true propositions. I don't see the Bible as just a collection of propositions. It is very much more than that.

MARGARET: It is the wrong point, but I wouldn't want to say that I don't accept the inerrancy of scripture. It is just not a word I would use.

ELAINE: Yes, that is what I feel, too. So there are some debates which don't concern me either as a woman or as an evangelical living now rather than fifty years ago. I don't suppose they concern the majority of other evangelical biblical scholars either.

There are some debates where I sit comfortably, and some where, again, as a feminist, I really have alarm bells ringing, not because of what the Bible says, but because of what people have made it mean. That has been the difficulty. Often it has been easier to deal with the sticky bits in the Hebrew scriptures, because Christians have cheerfully referred to these as the legacy from the Jewish tradition, not the Christian tradition.

MARGARET: It is such a delicate thing, isn't it? We used to bash on about how wonderful Jesus was, because these silly old Jews got it all wrong and then Jesus came along and put them all right. Suddenly you wake up to the fact of how anti-Semitic that approach is.

But still there is a sense of the Old Testament being brought to fulfilment, and therefore not standing sufficiently on its own.

ELAINE: I think we need just as much discernment in reading the Old Testament as the New. For instance, we need to recognize that what we read in Judges is different from what we read in Isaiah. There is a different feel, different mode, different nuances in it.

Again the key is hermeneutics – tapping into the right ways of approaching the Bible and of interpreting what particular chapters or passages mean.

One of the most difficult passages is Judges 19, the rape of the concubine.

MARGARET: Can you recall that story, as you did so vividly at that evening at Greenbelt?

ELAINE: A man goes to pick up his concubine because she has deserted him and gone back to her father, and he leaves all his other wives and goes to pursue her. The father manages to delay him for several days, but eventually the man is off with his concubine. Travelling back to his home they have to rest the night, and they avoid all the hostile territory and come to their home country. One of the locals in the market square kindly offers them hospitality. But hardly have they settled down for the night before a group of brigands come to demand that the guest has sex with them.

I still think the response of the host is breath-stopping: 'Don't do this to my guest, this is a slur on my hospitality. Here, have my virgin daughter instead, or his concubine.' There is no other way of reading this except to deduce that women may be sacrificed sexually if the alternative is homosexual rape.

So they take the concubine and rape her all night and drop her back next morning. Then the host and the guest get up and the man announces to his concubine that he is about to leave, but she can't move because she is dead. So he saddles her on his ass and takes her home, cuts her into twelve pieces and sends her remains round the tribes of Israel.

MARGARET: What does that mean?

ELAINE: That this is an outrage which he has suffered. The tribe responsible has treated him in a way that violates what is his, namely his concubine. There is some suggestion that this shouldn't have happened to her as well, but that does not get much attention in the text.

I've often got people I've taught to study that, especially when they are the kind who argue that hermeneutics is largely unnecessary, because it's quite clear what the Bible says. So I set the question, 'Well, what does the Bible say about marriage?' They all want to tell me that the Bible says that there is headship in marriage, and that the man is the head of the wife. 'Oh good,' I say, 'so let's read this, then, because here is an obvious picture of headship.' And they all sit stunned. Because they don't want this to be a picture of headship.

Then they say, 'Ah, but you have got to have better hermeneutics than that.' I say, 'Oh, so we do need hermeneutics?' Once you employ hermeneutics there, you also have to be prepared to employ it elsewhere: in Pauline passages, the Gospels, and everywhere else.

So it is actually quite a good way into helping people to have a little bit more depth in their Bible reading.

MARGARET: There is a bit like that in Genesis 19 as well, isn't there? When Lot gives hospitality to two angels in Sodom, and the locals turn up and want to bugger the angels. And Lot says, 'Don't do that, have my two daughters, they are virgins. I'll bring them out to you, and you can do with them what you please.'

But even in the ten commandments you get that kind of attitude reflected: 'Thou shalt not covet thy neighbour's property, thou shalt not covet thy neighbour's wife.' Nothing about 'Thou shalt not covet thy neighbour's husband.'

ELAINE: The ten commandments are given into a very patriarchal tradition. A lot of the deuteronomic laws give a different value to men and to women, to boy children and to girl children. This is represented all the time in different kinds of sacrifice and different kinds of birthing processes. There is no doubt about it, men are valued more in monetary and in social terms. We have to admit, too, that even with all the hermeneutical help we can get, there are some stories in the Old Testament which depict women in very oppressive situations. I like Phyllis Trible's idea that we need to read these, not to recover women's history, but simply in memoriam, to hear what women suffered.

MARGARET: And yet, with all that, the Old Testament writers still come out with these occasional pieces of beautiful poetry about God being like a mother, that we recalled when we were talking about God and the Trinity. There is the famous one about 'Can a mother forget her child?' and, towards the end of Isaiah, likening Israel to a child and God to the mother.

ELAINE: Yes, motherhood was always important. But I think the overall picture is not of a tradition where women were despised.

In the Old Testament there are strict rules about defiling women, and the responsibility for rape is clearly the man's and he must do what he can to restore the woman and her family (Leviticus 19:20–2; Deuteronomy 22:28). These laws are patriarchal but they are also quite protective.

It depends whether or not you can take patriarchy in any form as to how difficult you find those passages. If you accept that there can be 'benign' forms of patriarchy then you'll be less troubled by them. It's interesting that in Israel today, among the orthodox Jews, women have their own status. There is more of an argument now to allow women to be trained in Torah and be accepted among the rabbinic groups. But the high position for women at home remains, and that carries the huge responsibilities of maintaining belief and faithfulness into the next generation. Judaism has always been transmitted through the home. Even today, shabbat prayers incorporate the praise of the woman in Proverbs 31.

MARGARET: I would say, overall, whatever the difficulties, one continues to find tremendous consolation in the scripture. It is full of affirming and beautiful passages that make you feel God can be tough at times, but nonetheless we are held in very loving arms.

The sadness is when someone like Daphne Hampson says that she had to stop reading the Bible because she found it too painful. What does one say to that?

ELAINE: You find it painful if you read the Bible via the culture which presents it badly. In other words, if the people that you know in the church represent the negative things in the Bible, then there seems to be no way out of the pain except by rejecting the lot. I meet many women who are precisely in that place.

But my experience with people who love the Word and try to live it with humility is a very positive one. They bring the Bible alive. I would never let go of it. Some of the pain is still there, but by and large most of it is very liberating.

I did a series of sermons not long ago on the theme of 'the bride', starting with Hosea and some of the prophets and going right through to Revelation. I found it very stimulating. It raises questions like: what is it like for a man to be part of the bride of Christ? The image is in reverse, as it were, where men need to wrestle with what it is to be included in the feminine. What does it say about their masculinity and all the things about masculinity that current culture treasures?

The humiliation that Hosea goes through to try and woo his wife back can be read as a picture of the humiliation that God goes through in order to get his bride back. And although the husband – God – has all the power, actually he grovels in the dirt. He wears his heart so patently on his sleeve, and really humiliates himself before this bride who doesn't care, goes off with other lovers and is adulterous.

It is a very demeaning image of the bridegroom – of God – who tries to prevent his wife from getting to her lovers so that she might think of him instead. He acts with so little pride, almost without dignity, to try to get her back, because of love. I found it spoke very much of the emptying of God, the giving up of power, and the taking on of whatever it takes.

I ended with that passage from Revelation, 'The Spirit and the bride say, "Come".' It is a wonderfully inclusive invitation: 'Come.' The Spirit and the bride echo the invitation from almighty God to the wedding feast. It is one of the most delicious invitations in the whole of scripture.

MARGARET: Maybe to experience that symbol properly one needs to take it in a patriarchal sense, because now we have the idea of marriage as an equal partnership, we no longer 'love, honour and obey'. We don't become equal to God in our relationship, but it is more like that old one in which the wife is precious and beautiful and cherished and respected, but still the man's property. And that is actually a rather beautiful way of thinking ourselves honoured by God.

ELAINE: That's an interesting point. I couldn't see this as alienating for women. By the time we get to that point, there is nothing but liberation: nothing but a tingling excitement at being in the presence of God, who loves and invites and makes all things possible.

Ten

THE NEW TESTAMENT

MARGARET: Looking now at the New Testament, let's remember the question we started with – whether the Bible is the top source, or whether the Bible is the expression of the tradition, and so subject to selection and distortion. Is the really important thing what was written down? Or what actually happened?

Similarly, we have the question of how Jesus actually behaved towards women. Was there a lot more going on between him and the women than is reported? From the glimpses we have, there must have been so much that is left out. Therefore, one recognizes an inevitable bias in the evangelists, just as we are all biased.

ELAINE: Evangelicalism holds together the sense of twin authorship, that God wrote this and men wrote this. And it does that without any apparent difficulty. The New Testament is both God's truth which holds for all time and the expression of a developing Christian tradition, written down by men.

We have always accepted that what we have got in the New Testament is what we most need. Other writings might have been interesting too, but we don't have them. We don't have much of the early biography of Christ and we don't have the letters from the early churches to the apostles. They would have been fascinating to read. But they are not essential. What we do have tells us what we need to know about Christ's redemptive work and our salvation.

Of course, we have to ask about the alleged male bias. If a male bias is there, how important is it? Even more, is this bias God's or man's? That's the big issue for evangelical feminists.

We probably first need to ask what is meant by 'bias'. Sometimes the word is used to mean a deliberate distortion of reality, but when I talk about bias I mean something more like 'perspective' or 'prism'. Truth is there, but it is mediated to us largely through the incidents, teachings and insights written down by men.

Even so, God still speaks to women through the text in a way that includes them fully. In parts of the New Testament, especially in the Gospels, it is obvious that a lot of the stories are women's stories. The men wrote them down, but they are women's stories. At one level it barely matters who wrote them down, because the truth about God's inclusion of women is out.

Even from the texts we have it is obvious that Jesus has good relationships with women. Take the story of the woman at the well from John 4. (This is a good example, too, of a woman's story because only the woman was present.) Jesus is alone, thirsty, by a well without the means of getting water, and he asks a woman there for a drink. We find that she is a Samaritan woman, married five times and now 'living in sin'. The disciples were embarrassed when they returned and found Jesus in a conversation with her, and the story is told against them to some extent. At first, events like these seem almost incidentals to the main text, but they are very powerful indeed once you start to see them.

MARGARET: This reminds me of a wonderful image that Carla Ricci uses in her book, translated from the Italian, called

Mary Magdalene and Many Others (Burns and Oates, 1994). In her introduction she says that the presence of women in the Gospels is like an underground stream, which every so often comes up to the surface. From those little glimpses you can tell that the women have been there all along, and it is maddening that we cannot now recover more about them.

She draws attention particularly to Luke 8:3, the women who travelled with Jesus – Mary Magdalene and Joanna and Susanna and the rest. And also that bit in Matthew about the women at the cross, the women who had followed him from Galilee. Those personal details of Jesus with women are so beautiful that you have to be twisted not to get an overall sense of the value and affirmation Jesus gives to women. He doesn't value and affirm them by saying 'what you are doing is wonderful, you are in your right role and this is where your dignity lies'. He opens the doors and says, 'Come out of the kitchen, come and sit at my feet and study my words, like students are meant to do with rabbis.'

ELAINE: Once you see it, you can't miss it. But somehow the truth has been distorted by the traditions we have had, and we have invited women to go back into the very bondages that they are liberated from in the Gospels. The evangelical tradition has used the Bible in order to do that, and the Catholic tradition has used the church in order to do that. What to each of us has been the most important part of God's revelation has become that which cripples women again. I find it sobering that people take something so precious, and use it against Christ's freedom for women.

MARGARET: There are the two aspects, aren't there? The very evident breaking of the rules and taking people more into the inner circle, on the one hand, which is so affirming for women. But on the other hand, you have those who bash on about the apostles being twelve men.

Then that is put to quite illegitimate uses, like 'therefore only men can be priests', which is a complete non sequitur. First, because the apostles were not priests and priests are not apostles, and second, because there is no consideration of why non-Jews can be ordained, or non-fishermen, or whatever.

But even having seen through the absurdity of that argument against women's ordination, I still feel a sad puzzlement, you know, just very slight, that the twelve were men.

ELAINE: Working on a BBC script recently on the women at the cross (Radio 4, Good Friday 1996), it is interesting how the twelve who were men actually come over rather shabbily in a whole range of ways. But the women, who were not part of the twelve but were very much there all the way through, come over as incredibly different, even when the story is told by men.

MARGARET: Those passages about 'silly old disciples, they got it wrong' are always about the men. The ones who ran away were men. Nothing but good is spoken of the women.

It is amazing how new all this is. I mean, what we are saying may have been said lots of times, but it has only been said lots of times over the last ten years or fifteen years. In the seventies I wasn't yet aware of anyone saying, 'Look at the Gospels and you will see that Jesus is breaking with convention.' It was just beginning in the States, but it hadn't filtered through very far.

ELAINE: Dorothy Sayers did it earlier, the author of the radio play *The Man Born To Be King*. In a talk she gave in 1938, 'Are Women Human?', she says Jesus never nagged at women or patronized them, 'never made arch jokes about them, never treated them either as "The women, God help us!" or "The ladies, God bless them!" '. She says: 'There is no act, no sermon, no parable in the whole Gospel that borrows its pungency from female perversity; nobody could possibly guess from the words and deeds of Jesus that there was anything "funny" about women's nature.'

MARGARET: My uncle was Jesus in *The Man Born To Be King*, Robert Speaight, the actor.

But in a way, the most difficult passages of scripture for women are the early church ones.

ELAINE: Yes, they are, especially some of the Pauline letters. There's not much highlighting of women in Acts, either, the focus is definitely on male evangelists. There are, of course, some notable women, like Priscilla and Dorcas, who were obviously out there working hard and highly respected in the early church but who don't get majored on. But nor do we hear about large numbers of the men either, or they fade out, like Barnabas. People move out of orbit, as it were. Acts focuses on the key players, and we see the others as they come into focus with them, like Priscilla, who was a tent maker with Paul.

But it's a riveting, exciting account of the early church and the Holy Spirit. And there is nothing negative about women in Acts. The parts they play they play well.

MARGARET: And there is consolation to be found in the struggle against racism in Acts, so that even if the women issue isn't thought out as such, the issue of discrimination between peoples is, over the role of the gentiles, and even over the Ethiopian eunuch. So one can find parallels and echoes.

But then one way that we have of coping with the Pauline letters – I don't know if I go along with this, but I have no better theory – is that the authentic early church tradition was the emancipation of women, and then a conservative backlash came in, which was not from St Paul himself. And so you get interpolations in some Pauline letters. That is Elisabeth Schüssler Fiorenza's theory, isn't it?

That raises an interesting question, again going back to where we started with the authority of scripture. Does it make any difference in terms of authority whether it was Paul who said it or someone else? Do we take it on Paul's authority, or do we take it on God's authority because it is God's word? Is it relevant who wrote it?

But that is one of the theories, isn't it, that Paul as such was actually very liberated? He talks of Junia as an apostle, and there is a suggestion that probably this was a woman, or at least the name appears to be feminine. And he talks of Phoebe the deacon, in the same chapter, Romans 16. And of Priscilla and Aquila, who are nearly always called Priscilla and Aquila – wife before husband – rather than Aquila and Priscilla.

All this suggests that Paul gave women tremendous freedom. As apostles, as deacons, as leaders of house churches. So the suggestion is that the other, anti-women bits were written in over the top, by people trying to distort the Christian message. Now I don't see how an evangelical can swallow that.

ELAINE: I don't think I'd want to swallow it. Probably most scholars agree now that Romans, Corinthians, Galatians, Ephesians and Thessalonians were written by Paul, but that Timothy and Titus are up for grabs.

Then nobody really knows who wrote Hebrews, of course. There is an argument it might even be Priscilla. I don't know that it holds water, but it is a nice idea.

MARGARET: Well, everyone seems to agree that it wasn't Paul. I think it's a marvellous epistle.

ELAINE: It is. It is certainly somebody who is trying to reach the Jewish Christians in a very powerful way. So the human author is secondary to the fact that these writings are in the Bible.

But even if Paul did write the pastoral epistles, and Paul's name is on them, it is not an insurmountable problem for evangelicals in terms of the feminist issue. You have to see them in the context of all the other things Paul says and does on gender. And there could have been good reasons in the context of that church why he restricts women there while still holding to his central principle of Galatians 3:28.

A similar thing happens with the Jewish–gentile divide. In Galatians and Acts, Paul is vehement about not circumcising the gentile believer because there is no need – we were talking about this last time. In Acts, the church fights over the question, and they go to the Jerusalem court over it. Then, even though he is so committed and such a radical liberator, Paul has Timothy circumcised (Acts 16:1–3).

So what was going on? Either Paul preaches what he doesn't practise, or we need a different hermeneutic. You say instead: well, Paul is like the rest of us; every now and again he has to back off his own principles because the church isn't ready, isn't mature. There are other principles at stake.

In this case, making Timothy acceptable to the Jewish waverers – people who are still legalistic – was more important than holding out for the principle of non-circumcision. So he is sacrificing the liberation of some, and doing so fairly deliberately, because of hang-ups in the church.

So why shouldn't that be true on the whole issue of women? And once you allow the possibility of that, then the

Bible stays intact. It is still authoritative, still the word of God, but we read what Paul says in a deeper context, a bigger picture, the picture where, as you say, Paul is affirming women, and they do all kinds of things, including running house churches.

MARGARET: How do you, as an evangelical, deal with those who quote at you the text about 'the husband is the head of the wife just as Christ is the head of the church' (Ephesians 5:23)?

ELAINE: I smile and wonder why they need to quote it. But exegetically I always want to know what the context of the whole passage is about. Why is Paul writing this letter and to whom? What is going on in the church at the time? The problem with much evangelical reading of pastoral theology is that we often lift something out of context and then dole it out as though that solves everything.

For me there have to be questions and a process of understanding. A bit of scripture is quoted and the first question is: 'Oh, that's very interesting, what is that about? Is it a letter, a psalm, law, or a bit of prophecy or whatever?' So identifying the kind of literature is a first step.

OK, so it is a letter. Well, a letter from whom, to whom, and about what? And what do the words mean today? When Paul uses a word, *kephale* for example, what has he got in mind? He uses the word sometimes to mean 'head' as distinct from 'tail', or the 'head' of a coin – 'Whose head is this?' – and sometimes (and I think in these passages) it means 'head' as distinct from 'body', as we grow up into Christ who is our head when we are the body of Christ. And so Paul's use of *kephale*, head, when he is not using it to mean the thing on top of our bodies, is metaphoric, and the important question is: 'What does the metaphor mean?'

I am now bewildered when evangelicals continue to take a word like 'head' and add something called 'ship' on the end of it, and everybody talks about 'headship'. Suddenly, out of a perfectly nice Greek word, a whole theological construct emerges with a very strong meaning that is used to keep women in place. It is the most appalling kind of hermeneutic. It is so important not to build a theology on a metaphor.

Back to that particular verse, 'the husband is the head of the wife just as Christ is the head of the church'. Even that isn't straightforward, because the passage you've been looking at is about the unity of man and woman in marriage and the sense of oneness. Paul is talking to the Ephesian church about relationships in the church, and he chooses three distinct relationships: husband and wife, children and parents, slaves and masters. And he has something to say about each of these.

Now why is he bothering with those relationships? I think those who see this as instructions on keeping universal authority structures are hopelessly out of date. They can't be universal, because we now don't have slavery and we know it was a bad thing. So what Paul was saying in that case was a temporary expedient. It's much more to do with keeping the church together in difference.

The passage on husbands and wives is in the context of Christ's love for the church. And that is the big issue. Christ didn't love the church in the sense that he was the boss of the church, but he loved the church in a self-sacrificial, giving, no-holds-barred way. He loved the church by getting on the ground and washing the disciples' dirty feet, and by going to the cross. And it draws love back in return.

So to parallel husband-love with Christ's love is very demanding. As a picture of headship, it is very different from the one often conveyed. And yet that is what I think the passage really is about. It is about the union of a husband and wife together, their closeness, and also the sense of mutual sacrifice, mutual love, mutual care.

MARGARET: So we've got a simile, or a metaphor, or an analogy.

ELAINE: And instead of taking the thing that it is actually saying about God, it is taking the bit that it is not saying, and turning that into a doctrine. Which is, I am afraid, what some evangelicals do when they bring to the text certain kinds of structures and ideas about God, and impose on the text.

Then they step back and say, 'We are people of the Book, we take all our theology from the Bible.' But sometimes they bring theology to the Bible, put it there and then take it away with them. And then they wonder why you have movements out of evangelicalism, people who no longer feel that way.

MARGARET: What about the problems in Timothy?

ELAINE: Timothy is the epistle with the heaviest passage against women preaching or speaking publicly. It is where it says: 'I permit no woman to teach or to have authority over a man; she is to keep silent' (1 Timothy 2:12).

MARGARET: Does it make it easier for you if it is not Paul who wrote it?

ELAINE: The problem has been that what the Bible says, God says, and therefore if the Bible says women have to be silent, God says women have to be silent. That is not really held very seriously now because we recognize that hermeneutics are involved in understanding what God says. But if Paul wrote it, and if he wrote it to Timothy who was his fellow worker – all these 'if's – then Timothy was already the fellow worker of Priscilla, who was already teaching and who already had authority among Christians (Acts 18). So that means that Paul can't have been meaning, 'No women ever', because one woman was doing it, at least one, and you only need one to defeat the principle.

And then you say, 'Well, maybe Paul didn't know,' and that's daft, because clearly Paul did know it. 'Maybe Paul didn't approve' – well, he did approve of Priscilla, and sends greetings to her at the end of the second letter to Timothy (and at the end of Romans and 1 Corinthians). So if Paul wrote the passage it is not a universal prohibition on women. And for most evangelicals the big issue is about whether Paul wrote this and how it holds together as Pauline doctrine.

MARGARET: The next question is, how far do you go and how fast, when people are at different points in their relation to feminism, because you can only go as far as people will let you.

ELAINE: I think you go as fast as you can and as far as you can, so for me this is not even a question. With those people who are saying, 'No, no, this is all anti-biblical, anti-scriptural,' you have to bring to their attention both new and often very old biblical exegesis, because they think they're the ones who've got the traditional evangelical exegesis and we're all upstarts.

Who was it who said, centuries ago, that in order for something to be real it has to be historical, so anything new must be wrong? Maybe it was Pythagoras. There's a tremendous revulsion towards anything that sounds like a departure from ancient ways of wisdom. So a lot of the time we have to show people this isn't a departure. This is the gospel, this is biblical reality. So we do the homework and the footwork. And I find that now probably the most tedious, because that's what I was doing fifteen years ago. Then it was very exciting because I was learning from it and a lot of other people were getting very excited about it. Now I feel people ought to have moved on a bit. So to go back and do it again...

MARGARET: ...gets boring, rehearsing the same arguments.

ELAINE: Yes, and it is still true but you feel you ought now to be applying the Bible, moving on rather than going back and putting the same passages – the same 1 Timothy 2, 1 Corinthians 11 and Ephesians 5 – under the microscope. For me the argument's done, it's won, it's finished. But we have to keep going back, too, because unless people can believe that something is biblical they're not going to shift at all. I understand that, it's not a problem to me.

But then the question is: what makes them decide? For there is a group who only identify the biblical with their own opinions about the Bible. They really do see themselves as the only authority on biblical truth, so being biblical means agreeing with me. You're probably not going to win them over, so how far do you go? Well, do what you can but probably stop early, shake their hands and pray, and work with other people who are more likely to bend or change or listen.

MARGARET: I am very aware of Daphne Hampson's critique – that in the end Christianity is based on the Bible and can never be released of this male bias. That is the real question. One wants to answer it by supplementing the Bible, you see, and that is where I find help in the idea of the ongoing people of God, who can go on writing their history, not quite with scriptural authority but still in continuity.

ELAINE: Yes, that is certainly one way forward, and the other way forward is to go back to the original text and see what it would have sounded like had it been written with the language that we use today. That is what the inclusive versions are trying to do, largely. So where it says 'brother', to translate it as 'brother or sister' actually makes massive impact, because the overall flavour is different.

We have had correspondence on the *Women's Study New Testament* I have been involved in editing (Marshall Pickering, 1995) from women who said, 'We just didn't realize the Bible was so friendly to us.' We haven't changed the text at all, just used the inclusive version, adding footnotes and highlighting areas you could miss quite easily.

MARGARET: Actually, I have got an interesting story about inclusive language. Yesterday I led a little prayer workshop with students at Oxford. We were praying on Matthew's temptations, and in the sharing afterwards, one girl was saying she focused on this phrase: 'one does not live by bread alone'; and 'one' meant so much to her. She was praying over this word 'one'. And I pointed out to her that the familiar translation has always been 'man does not live by bread alone', and there are plenty of people who would say you were interfering with the text by changing it.

It is difficult, it is almost a losing battle, when you start putting in inclusive language, because there is no answer as to how far to go. It is quite difficult to know in a lot of instances whether it is better to use an inclusive form or not.

ELAINE: When might it not be?

MARGARET: Suppose you are translating the feeding of the five thousand, and you put 'men and women' into Mark 6 or

Luke 9. Then you read the parallel text in Matthew 14, and find out there were 'five thousand men, not including women and children'. And I have seen other instances where I have really wondered if the women were included or not.

The 'sons' of God is difficult. Christ is the Son of God, and you may lose something by saying we are adopted 'children'. I think that is why you need both versions. There is always value in having an absolutely literal version, and value also in having a much more adapted version.

Another serious objection is that you are losing resonances from the tradition, as, for example, with the 'son of man' if you translate that as 'child of humanity' or even 'son of humanity', and lose the echoes of Daniel 7:13. But then you only lose something from the tradition if you keep 'son of man' for the Old Testament translation and have a different phrase in the New Testament.

ELAINE: The problem of losing is that we lose anyway. We have lost so much in translation because we don't live in those times. Those words don't mean what they did then. We don't have that kind of culture, we don't have those inheritance patterns. We don't even have that depth of awareness of sin in society, knowing what it is to disobey a holy God.

Because we have lost so much, the idea of rigidly holding on to words which somehow symbolize all that we have lost, and bringing them into our culture as though all we have lost is those particular words, makes little sense.

I bemoan that we have lost all these things. I regret that we haven't got a society and a culture that fears God, where all these things mean something very deep. But there are things also to rejoice about, like the move away from a heavily patriarchal society. God is still with us.

So the question for me is how we can make the scripture accessible to people now. And how much we are prepared to let go of things that we will lose in a newer, inclusive translation rather than having to explain to people: 'Well, it really meant this.' If we could always explain the text rather than change words like 'son' it would be better. But there comes a point where the people who read it on their own for the first time are going to find these words alienating.

So I think you are right, we have to be working on both fronts.

Eleven

THE MOTHER OF JESUS

♀ MARGARET: When I wrote *Six New Gospels* (Geoffrey Chapman, 1994) I had to make myself look at the mother of Jesus properly for the first time. Before then I had found this a very difficult subject, particularly since writing *Motherhood and God*, because the whole point of that book was to see God as our mother, and yet my Catholic upbringing had taught me to see Mary of Nazareth as our mother. So Mary had siphoned off all the maternal imagery that I wanted to apply to God.

That is one reason for my reluctance. The other is that the image of Mary that was presented to me at convent school was so unappetizing. She was supposed to be a womanly model for us, but she was not the sort of model that I admired. She seemed terribly soppy, a model of virginity and meekness and patience and service, and all covered up, rather like a nun. She seemed to have almost the equivalent of a convent enclosure, being confined to Nazareth. The men in the Gospels travelled about with Jesus, but the role of Our Lady was to be holy and stay at home.

Even the virginity thing I still find difficult. I accept it because I accept the creeds of the church, but with the proviso that this is something that I don't quite understand. The difficulty for me is that if we look at a married woman today and hear she has taken a vow of virginity, that is not something that we admire. So I could admire Mary more if she were not a virgin.

Yet I think the point of the virginity is that it is meant to help people admire Mary more – to make her more pure. I want to keep that sense of her not having lost virtue, without having her demoted in my eyes as a woman who wasn't a proper wife. The idea that motherhood is better if you don't have sex beforehand runs right contrary to our understanding of sexual theology today.

I have been helped a little by the new feminist interpretation that sees the virginity as a way in which a woman keeps her personal integrity and does not become dependent on a man. That makes sense for me. So I like to see Mary as a wife who maintains her independence – and that's a mind-boggling new way of approaching Mary.

Then she is the sister who proclaims revolution in the Magnificat – 'He has brought down the powerful from their thrones ... and sent the rich away empty.' We haven't just invented that, it has been developed over the last ten or twenty years by liberation theology.

And then there is a new strand which I am quite excited about and which I have only really noticed in this last week, while I have been preparing to talk to you. Look at almost any picture of Mary at the annunciation: what is she doing when she is interrupted by the angel? She is reading a book. It is more common than the lily of purity as a symbol. So we have a mother who reads books.

I began to touch on that tradition of Mary's literacy in *Six New Gospels*, though I hadn't yet registered the prevalence of the book symbol in the annunciation. All I picked up on was the pictures of her with her mother, Anna (who of course is not in the Bible and therefore this is something that as an evangelical you won't feel so comfortable about). In the iconography you have a great tradition of Anna teaching Mary to read.

So we have the woman in the family being the booky one, while Joseph is the practical one, the carpenter. This is a whole new way of looking at the holy family, and it is there in tradition, if not in scripture.

As a Catholic, I start with a backlog of sickly Marian piety which I find distasteful, and probably you do too – and I am very sympathetic to the Protestant objection that our whole Mariology has been built on a fiction which is not in the scriptures. But then I come back to the Catholic tradition and I find things in the iconography which make new sense to me, and then I am glad to be a Catholic and have this extra source to draw on, tradition as well as scripture.

It is what I would call *ben trovato* theology, because we don't have any proof of it, it's what seems appropriate. I think Mariology always has been built on what would be appropriate for the mother of Jesus, so Mary is imagined according to the current ideal of womanhood. The medieval formula was *potuit, decuit, fecit* – God could do it, it was fitting to do it, so God did it.

That gets dangerous if you think you have found a historical figure, but I think it can still mean something. One just has to be aware of what is scripture and what is tradition, and know when one is drawing from the idea of fittingness rather than from history.

ELAINE: To start with my tradition, I suppose as an Anglican I was never used to seeing pictures, images, statues of Mary at all. They simply didn't feature in my church background. In stained glass Mary popped up, but she was usually by the cross or else looking at the small infant Jesus. She was just like any other woman, there was nothing special about Mary. And that for me felt perfectly natural, and I am still very comfortable with that.

I have always enjoyed the references to Mary in the scriptures. The gospel writers who call upon her virginity go to pains to imply fulfilment of the Old Testament prophecies, and I have never had any problem with believing in the virgin birth. When people ask me to explain it to them, I always think that is a daft request. How can I possibly? God didn't take me into his confidence. So I don't have any problems with the fact that I can't explain it, either genetically or in terms of chromosomes. That is not an issue for me. It is a mystery, the details of which haven't been disclosed to us. The fact has but the process hasn't. Many miracles are like that.

So none of those things have been problems in terms of belief. And yet I have always, since I was a young girl, had questions about why she is so important within Catholicism. Whenever I travelled on the Continent I would see paintings or sculptures of Mary, and most of them have been quite exciting. I love the Leonardo cartoon, the Michelangelo pietas and many others (except for the very pious ones with spikes coming out of her head, which have always given me a shiver!). But sometimes the rather run-of-the-mill statues in some churches can seem more menacing than liberating.

What I have always felt comfortable with is Mary as a mother. Mothering Sunday has always featured Mary as a role model for mothering. But it is motherhood through suffering which has been conveyed in the Bible. As I have grown older I have appreciated that more fully.

You see a lot of the anxiety and love mingled together in the gospel. For example, there is the story of Jesus disappearing on the journey back home and he is found in the temple talking to the wise leaders and the scribes. Mary's anxiety over that is palpable, and she goes to pains to find out where he is. Then there are the long excursions where he is preaching and she and his brothers are trying to see him, presumably to get him back home. I love the biblical stories about Mary because they picture someone with whom I can identify in a very full way. I would be like that, probably more neurotic and more anxious.

I can't ignore the sheer level of suffering she must have gone through, so even the swooning Marys of the paintings, even though they look a bit coy, make sense to me. They are trying to give us a glimpse of what it was like for this woman to suffer, and that is incredibly poignant. None of that has ever been an issue. It has been a help.

MARGARET: And Mary's suffering has a basis in the scriptures in the sword piercing the soul (Luke 2:35).

ELAINE: Yes, that's right.

But Catholic Marian doctrines have always frankly mystified me. Until recently I wondered where they came from, and why they were there. Why did the church insist that Mary remained a virgin when, in the Gospels, she had other children? The conclusion that they are nephews or other family members has never rung true for me. I mean, what can be gained theologically from her being a perpetual virgin? In fact, when the text says Joseph didn't know her 'until she had borne a son' (Matthew 1:25), the implication is that after that he did know her – in other words, they had sex.

My readings of the scriptural passages about her virginity have never led me to believe anything other than that this was a special situation because there was something very special about this child. The focus is on the child, the incarnation, and Mary's virginity is, if you like, the process through which this happened, but it is nothing to do with virginity as such. It is nothing to do with sex, and it is certainly nothing to do with taking a vow of celibacy during marriage. That would be a far cry from what is written in either the Gospels or the epistles.

I agree that the paintings of the Anna–Mary relationship present something quite lovely. And it is not true that evangelicals reject anything that is not in scripture: there are all kinds of things that we don't know because scripture doesn't cover them, and we are just as happy as anyone else to speculate on what might have happened. Some people write dramatic narratives exploring all kinds of possibility. But we regard the scriptural accounts as true, and anything else simply as speculative. They are no less fascinating, we just don't put any weight on them. We don't need to believe them or act upon them, they are just interesting possibilities.

MARGARET: I would go along with that. When I see a book in the pictures of the annunciation and I say 'symbol of literacy', I accept that is speculation. I don't for a moment think, just because there are a lot of paintings showing Mary with a book, that it proves she really was like that.

But it is a nice idea and an idea I want to work with. It is almost as though you have two parallel strands, the male theologians saying, 'Isn't Mary wonderful because she was so modest and she had no ambitions and she never wanted to be a priest.' And then alongside that you have the painters showing her educating herself, presenting the Mary of the intellectual life. It is such an unusual thing for a woman to be doing. Even today. Yet I don't know of anyone who has noticed this.

ELAINE: No, I haven't noticed it.

MARGARET: Apart from the annunciations, there are also paintings of mother and child that continue the theme of

Mary reading a book. There is an unfinished painting ascribed to Michelangelo in the National Gallery, which has the boy Jesus trying to stop her reading her book – I love that, because it is such a familiar experience for a mother. And there's a beautiful painting in the Prado in Madrid, by Bernard van Orley, where she is distracting the child with a red necklace and a pear while she is trying to read.

The holy family as a refugee family has been valuably re-emphasized in recent years, and it is good to find that the rest on the flight into Egypt has been a frequent theme for artists. The holy family had to flee in the middle of the night in such a hurry that we can imagine they had no papers. That speaks powerfully to our modern world refugee crisis.

So there are several great insights about Mary in terms of the option for the poor. There is the liberation Mary of the Magnificat, and there is the homeless Mary of the nativity, and there is the refugee Mary from the flight into Egypt. These are all precious rediscoveries of her in our day. She is an icon for the marginalized, and should rightly mean a lot to the poor of the world. But what is so wonderful is to find that she identifies with the poor, and yet at the same time she is a woman who reads books. So we hold the two in balance.

When I was in southern Spain last year, I found two striking images in Granada Cathedral showing Mary as a priest. There was the dead Christ on the altar, Mary behind dressed up elaborately, almost as though vested as a priest, the empty cross behind her and her arms out in a priestly gesture as though offering the sacrifice of the Mass. The only person who could truly say, 'This is my body, this is my blood.' I have never seen that anywhere else but in Granada.

A recurrent image is Mary as mother of the church, holding out a big cloak over all the little people. I am not sure if I like that image of Mary or not.

ELAINE: No, I don't like it at all. It is to some extent the cosmic mother.

MARGARET: Is it because she seems to be like a goddess?

ELAINE: Yes, I think so.

MARGARET: I think it has been a mistake of the Catholic Church to isolate those words from the cross, 'Behold your mother,' from their complement, 'Behold your son' (John 19:26–7). If Mary is given to the church as mother, we should also see the beloved disciple given to the church as son. Yet no one ever says that. I think the point of those words is to say that in Christ we have a new family which is the family of believers, and the old narrow family is broken down. It goes with all those sayings about leaving your father and mother and brothers and sisters for the sake of Christ (Matthew 19:29; Luke 14:26).

ELAINE: We haven't talked about the conflicts. What has always been interesting for me are those scriptural accounts where Jesus and his mother seem to be at odds.

It sometimes sounds almost rude when Jesus doesn't respond to her call but asks: 'Who are my mother and my sisters and brothers? Whoever does the will of God is my brother and sister and mother' (Mark 3:33–5). But I never take that as a rebuff, not even when a woman bursts out in the crowd and cries, 'Blessed is the womb that bore you and the breasts that nursed you,' and he replies, 'Blessed rather are those who hear the word of God and obey it' (Luke 11:27–8). I don't believe that is a rebuke of Mary, but a caution about the adulation of motherhood – even the motherhood of Mary herself.

What Jesus said also deliberately includes single women and men who have no family. That must have been important in those familial days when being part of a family gave you your identity. God doesn't look on our status in terms of whom we have produced, but upon our love for God and our preparedness to listen to God's truth.

So Mary becomes a means by which truth is communicated, even when the stories seem initially negative about her.

MARGARET: Jesus certainly tried to establish a certain distance from her, didn't he? I see that as the breaking away from your family into the freedom of the missionary life, and of course women were taken along as those missionaries, as we see in Luke 8. So if his mother was a stay-at-home woman – if she was and we don't know she was, but that is the way tradition has seen her – then that wasn't the only way in which women could be disciples.

ELAINE: How do you explain the bodily assumption? To me the problem is that this is close to old Greek paganism and the form–matter distinction, and the idea that somehow matter is wrong. Form or spirit or soul is the real reality, but we can't see it, feel it or touch it. It exists in the world of the beyond. But matter is unreal, and its very visibility is problematic because it is tactile, bodily, sensual and decaying all the time. It is somehow evil. Those influences on early Christianity have left a long legacy and whenever they emerge are awkward.

I wonder if that is why, in Catholic interpretation, Mary doesn't rot in the ground like the rest of us. She doesn't have a bodily ageing, rotting process, because matter is evil. But, because it is not her earthly body that is important; I don't see why she couldn't have just died and been buried. It is the resurrection of bodies that is going to be key.

MARGARET: I think Catholics would say very firmly that precisely what the assumption does is affirm the goodness of matter. It is the opposite of what you are saying. The body is so important that, instead of thinking Mary is in heaven spiritually, Catholics say she receives her resurrected body immediately. It happens first to her, as a promise to all of us that when we are fully resurrected in heavenly glory we will have our bodies.

ELAINE: That is a very different explanation.

MARGARET: I had another thought just in these past few days about the assumption, I don't know if there is any mileage in it. Mary is always physically very lovely and desirable – with big, rounded, bared breasts – maybe as a counterbalance to her untouchable chastity. Perhaps it is because she is so precious physically that she doesn't go stiff and cold but remains soft and warm, as her body is assumed into heaven.

The other thing to remember about the assumption is that this is a very ancient idea, because you sometimes get Protestants talking as though the Catholic Church made it up in the twentieth century. The beauty of it is its age.

ELAINE: And then I have struggled with the immaculate conception.

MARGARET: I think the doctrine has some problems, but when it was defined in 1854 the positive thing was that it was an affirmation of the laity, because this is what the people believed, you know, what the people wanted. And that has a nice side. We are all pro laity.

ELAINE: Explain that to me. Why is it a lay idea?

MARGARET: Emotions ran very high among those who thought Mary's honour was not being sufficiently recognized. There were secret societies where people swore to protect Mary's honour, sealing their oaths with their own blood. The argument was technically over a tiny theological nuance – whether Mary was conceived without original sin or whether she was first conceived and then cleansed of original sin. It seems an absurd thing to argue about. But somehow people associated that with honouring her.

One of the difficult things with Mariology is the immense mass of people for whom this woman is so precious.

ELAINE: And also liberating for a lot of women, I recognize that, too.

MARGARET: One doesn't want to undervalue that or tread on it, even though there are aspects of traditional Mariology that just make me go 'yuk'.

So how does one redeem that? I think this is where Mary of the Magnificat has been enormously helpful. The liberation theologians are so appreciative of popular devotion. If there is a local tradition of honouring Mary – and there always is – they would never say that it is wrong or unimportant, but they supplement it so that she is seen as a strong woman, an innovator, a woman who proclaims this extraordinary reversal of wealth and power. I think that is the right way forward, to discover new aspects to her without hurting anyone's belief.

ELAINE: But what does the immaculate conception mean? Because I never really understood this. Some people suggest it means she was conceived without sex.

MARGARET: No, it doesn't mean that. It means that from the precise moment of her conception she did not have the stain of original sin on her soul. That happened through the grace of Christ, even though it was previous in time. So she was never impure in any way.

Having said that, however, I went to a day conference at the National Gallery where there was a discussion of *The Kiss of Anna and Joachim at the Golden Gate* – which is associated with her conception, because they met and kissed there after a vision that Anna would have a child although she was old. One of the Catholics in the audience tried to dispel the confusion between a sexless conception and the immaculate conception, to which one of the art curators replied very sceptically that it was all very well to try to explain it away, but there was no doubt in his mind that the immaculate conception had been historically understood by many and interpreted through painting as a conception without sex.

ELAINE: That is how it was presented to me. I remember sitting down with one priest a long time ago who said, 'In order for her to be able to conceive Christ without sin, she had herself to be without sin. And so being conceived without sin, her conception was virginal.' Now that threw me and I asked, 'So sin is about sex?' 'No,' he said, and I was left feeling I had missed something.

It is the relationship between sex and sin which seems to be there in Marian dogmas, especially in the doctrine of her perpetual virginity. It is not so much a discussion about whether Mary could or did or would sin, although I happen to believe that she did, like anybody else, so, like everybody else, she needed Christ's redeeming grace in her life. If you are saying Christ's grace was mediated to her at the very beginning, I can understand that a little. But if that entailed that she had to be both virginally conceived and perpetually virginal, the discussion becomes too focused on sex.

MARGARET: You wouldn't find any theologian arguing that, that she was virginally conceived.

ELAINE: Phew! Of course, for a lot of people, even the virgin birth of Jesus is a problem. The argument is that because it is impossible for anyone to be a virgin and a mother, the church was presenting women with an absolutely impossible role model. Karen Armstrong insists that this was all because the Catholic Church was terrified of sex and particularly female sexuality, which is why priests are celibate.

So the only woman revered in the Catholic Church is herself a non-sexual woman, and Mary's asexuality is absolutely essential in order for her to have the position she has, and not to be a threat to men. Being a virgin mother means we can heap piety, respect and admiration on her, whereas ordinary mothers just leave people with loads of problems! How do you respond to those arguments?

MARGARET: They certainly say something to me. I have always disliked this singling out of her as being above everyone else. I have always found that a turn-off.

ELAINE: I have been impatient with it because it seems so out of kilter with the biblical account. So it has made me more open to the subversive analysis of Armstrong and others. But I don't want to see it that way, because I don't want to dismiss centuries of pious reverence of Mary and simply concede that she is made up by the church, and used to subdue women and chasten their sexuality. So I keep hoping there is another explanation.

I like what Alwyn Marriage says in *Lifegiving Spirit: responding to the feminine in God* (SPCK, 1989). As a Catholic, she describes what she believes about Mary and what she has had to reject. Discarding perpetual virginity, she goes on to say this rather lovely thing:

> My love and respect have nothing to do with whether Mary had sexual intercourse with her husband. I sincerely hope she did. I am not interested in whether or not she ever sinned in any way, for within the new dispensation sin is forgiven and therefore doesn't separate us from God. I can see no point in speculating on whether Mary died and decayed in the way we mortals do, with whether she received a special crown in heaven, or whether she intercedes for human beings with God. Such embellishments to history are the preserve of legend, not theology and prayer.
>
> The Mary whom I value in my heart and try to celebrate in my living is the ordinary woman who was open to the unexpected and unconventional, and who put her whole love and obedience to God above respectability. She is the one who listened more than she talked, who sang in joy and obedience to the will of God as she saw it making waves within her own life, and who, watching her child grow, was prepared to observe and ponder in her heart rather than rushing in to manipulate or control when things didn't go as she expected.

MARGARET: That's beautiful, the idea of her as 'an ordinary woman who was open to the unexpected and unconventional'. That is the annunciation moment. There is a prayer called the Angelus which we used to say every day when I was at school: 'The Angel of the Lord declared unto Mary, And she conceived by the Holy Ghost' – the Holy Spirit, we would say nowadays – 'Behold the handmaid of the Lord, Be it done to me according to thy word.' (I can't stand the translation of 'handmaid'.)

It is lovely to think in the middle of your day – twelve noon is the traditional time for the Angelus – you interrupt everything you are doing and you think of this other ordinary woman in the middle of what she was doing, with her other plans, and suddenly – boing! God comes in, changes all her plans, and she says, '*Fiat*, let it happen, let it be done.'

And then *fiat* becomes the essential mark of the Lord's Prayer: 'Thy kingdom come, thy will be done.' It's a re-expression of 'Let it be done to me according to thy word.'

ELAINE: Yes, that's right.

MARGARET: So she taught Jesus to pray, which is a lovely idea as well.

And then we all share something of Mary's vocation and become, in our own different ways and at our own different levels, God-bearers, people who let the Holy Spirit work through us, and who are unexpectedly, in the middle of our work, given unexpected tasks to do and invited to say 'Yes' to them.

ELAINE: Yes, it is the interrupted quality, as you say, the listening and the receiving, even though it breaks into the normal convention.

MARGARET: Another thing I wanted to pick up on, because I think it terribly important, is that Mary 'pondered these things in her heart', which we get twice at the beginning of

Luke (Luke 2:19, 51). I see that as a reminder that these traditions in the early chapters in Luke, insofar as they have a historical kernel, must have come from her, directly or indirectly.

If you take all that out, take Christmas out of Christianity, you are left with a dry abstract religion – words and deeds, sayings and acts – and it loses that sense of incarnation already present in the childhood and in the infancy, even in the womb. It loses the idea of salvation through presence. And this absolutely central tradition in theology comes from this one woman.

So she is one of the most important formative influences of theology, you know, comparable to St Paul. I find that an amazingly exciting idea. It comes through the principle of experience, treasured and pondered, remembered and reflected upon. And she is the one who has done it.

ELAINE: Yes. The early chapters of Luke have to be Mary's story because – certainly in the case of the annunciation – nobody else was there. So I think you are right in saying the pondering of these things in her heart, and then the passing on, is a vital part of biblical tradition.

MARGARET: It is the visit of the shepherds that she pondered in her heart, and then the finding in the temple. But I bet the presentation story comes from her as well. And probably the visitation, because by that time maybe Elizabeth was dead.

Nobody else that I know of has noticed this aspect of Mary – as a theologian, an innovator of experience-based theology. They just go on about a character who is wonderful because she is so passive and humble.

ELAINE: One thing we haven't discussed that has always been of enormous theological significance for me is Mary as a Jewish woman.

It has been easier to think of Mary as Jewish than almost anybody in the New Testament. She is a woman who goes through Jewish customs of betrothal, and she has to be part of the census. The business of going back to your father's town and lineage is significant. Mary straddles the bridge between the old and the new covenants, as a Jewish woman, born into the line of David, responding to the Torah and knowing with her family the covenant promises of God throughout the generations.

That comes out powerfully in the Magnificat. This is a God who remembers his faithfulness to Abraham and all his descendants: the Magnificat is a very Jewish prayer. Mary lives inside that, and she bears the covenant in her own body.

Far more important for me than any virginity or anything is this historical and racial significance, this lineage. The movement from the old, faithful, generational waiting and persistence and belief to the coming of the Messiah through Mary is something I have held in awe. It is the sense of being the one through whom God renews his covenant with the people. And not just her own people, but the gentiles and the whole world.

Twelve

THE PLACE OF MEN

ELAINE: If the place of men in all this is significant, the big question is: who decides what's the place of men? Christian feminism has usually assumed that women have the main say about what is the place of men. We've often been perceived as attempting to define for men what their place is, and when we've done that, I think we've made a mistake.

That has been to articulate the situation as we see it, inviting the men into our understanding of reality, and then asking what they're going to do about it. It's not surprising that some men have resented this idea that we are writing their agenda for them. What I'm interested in now is the number of men who are defining the issue for themselves.

The issue is about the inclusiveness of the gospel – the dignity of women and giving them a bigger place and more freedom within the church – but it's also about rediscovering masculinity in the light of post-feminism. There's all of that in the new male consciousness that you're getting in some parts of the church, which I find incredibly exciting. Those men who are already within the orbit, as it were, have done a lot of thinking already, but their thinking is on different lines from women.

There are, almost, four different kinds of men. There are the men who have thought this through with women, and have listened to the women's arguments, and then applied it to themselves in their own way, in a particularly male way or masculine way.

There are the men who have gone along with the women and are still fighting for the women's cause and the women's battle, and have never gone on to say, 'How does this apply to me?' in a self-conscious way. So they're still with the general fight.

Then there are the men who are right back at square one, feeling in principle this would be very nice and extremely jolly, but the church isn't ready for it yet: 'We're not actually ready to change structures but we think in principle this is significant.'

And then there are those men who have stopped before square one, saying, 'All this is unchristian or unbiblical or untraditional, and we're staying where we were before.'

Those four positions are all there within the church as a whole, and I can quite quickly spot, as an Anglican and as an evangelical Protestant, where men are in my spectrum. With Catholic men it's harder, because we're not dealing with the same backcloth.

I think the most dangerous group is probably the third group, the ones who say, 'Yes, we are completely with you on all of this, we do agree, we do understand,' but actually do absolutely zilch about it. In fact, if anything, they offer us more resistance and problems than those who say this is heresy.

MARGARET: That's fascinating, those four types at four different places along the road. In Catholic terms you would have a huge number at – now wait a minute, are Group 1 the ones who haven't started?

ELAINE: We'll start with Group 1, yes, let's make it a progress.

MARGARET: So Group 1 are the ones who haven't started. That would be a lot, obviously. Probably nearly all Catholic men who didn't fall into Group 1 would be in Group 2. But there is an extra factor there for Catholics. It's not just that they don't know what to do about it and they don't feel ready to try, but a lot – certainly as regards the clergy and bishops – would like more to be done but the constraints are such that they can't or daren't. I don't necessarily mean that critically, because if they are clergy or bishops and they do something about women, they risk losing their jobs. And is that the most helpful thing for women?

Personally, I think it's more helpful for women to have people in the episcopacy who sympathize and are ready to move when the moving is possible, than to have them removed. It's very rare for a bishop actually to be removed – though it did happen to the French bishop Jacques Gaillot, and it has effectively happened to one or two others – but they certainly have their careers stopped.

Now Group 3 – would that be men who, for example, would come to feminist liturgies, because they're fully in solidarity?

ELAINE: And in Anglican evangelicalism, if they were in positions of authority themselves they would make sure that they got women in positions of authority working alongside them. They would be actively promoting women in leadership in some way or other, and working with the whole breadth of women's gifts. That's the ones I see as Group 3.

MARGARET: I think there would be a fair number of Catholic men in ministry who would think they were in Group 3.

ELAINE: There is sometimes quite a thin line between 2 and 3.

MARGARET: Priests, for example, who work with women chaplains, though when you actually look at the reality the women are vastly inferior. I have in mind a particular example where the woman has five degrees and many years of experience, and she's serving as junior to a newer chaplain, a young priest. And the young priest has the top title and all the authority really, even apart from being able to celebrate the sacraments, which she can't do. He has an incomparably bigger and better room, for starters. If it came under the sexual equality legislation there'd be no doubt about it at all. But of course it doesn't, because not only is the church excluded but the crucial factor is that one's ordained and the other can't be.

Then I remember being at one of the Synods in Rome when they were talking about women, and various statements came out saying how important it was that women should play a fuller role in the church. And the question at the press conference put to the panel of carefully selected people who were going to give the Vatican line was: 'What do you think are the jobs in the Roman Curia which women could do?' And they came up with 'secretaries'.

There was a lot of rhetoric about the difference between the Marian and the Petrine role in the church – this is the idea of Hans Urs von Balthasar, which is very much the approved line in Rome at the moment, basically that women have a different kind of vocation, they're absolutely wonderful creatures...

ELAINE: Absolutely marvellous, yes.

MARGARET: ...but they're called to respond to the gospel in a different way.

But now, where on your 1, 2, 3, 4 would you put someone I very much admire, Jim Cotter? I think he has an enormous sensitivity to the feminine.

ELAINE: I think probably in Group 4, because he has done a lot of work looking at spirituality, including men's spirituality, as well as fighting for the whole liberation cause. That's the kind of thing I have in mind, though he has other agendas, as far as I understand them, from the ones that I'm particularly talking about.

MARGARET: Other agendas being the gay agenda.

ELAINE: Within evangelicalism there's a split-off between, on the one hand, those who are looking hard at the whole gender issue, with regard to both feminism and masculinity, from within orthodoxy and sexual ethics as they have been traditionally articulated, and, on the other, those who are doing it from a particular point of view because of the gay issue.

Once the two get fused then evangelicals can become afraid or wary or threatened, and one of the ways in which you can always either close down the debate or get a 'No' vote is just to say, 'If we do this what will follow? Will we be ordaining practising homosexuals?' That's an immediate turn-off, and because it has acted as a threat we've kept the issues as far separate as possible. I think they are two different issues, with different hermeneutics and different areas of debate.

MARGARET: The interesting thing about Jim Cotter's work, I think, is that one wouldn't know of the gay agenda from within his writings at all – at least, I haven't noticed any signs of it.

ELAINE: I'm sure you're right.

MARGARET: I know of it only from other sources. But what his prayers are all about is inclusivity. Primarily you feel the male-female inclusivity, because he avoids the male pronouns and has lots of female imagery and so on, but logically and philosophically it extends to other kinds of inclusivity too, like racial inclusivity.

ELAINE: Then there's the issue of the Promise Keepers – have you come across them?

MARGARET: Oh yes.

ELAINE: And where to put those is a big question.

MARGARET: Come on, say more about it.

ELAINE: In the United States they certainly started off at square one, because they came on an all-male ticket with stereotypes. But they've shifted a good deal. They're still on an all-male ticket, but now they're talking about much more inclusiveness and seeing women with equal dignity, so they've moved on to point 2.

Now what happens when they come into England? I had a comment on television, on the *Six O'Clock News*, and as soon as I got back I had the phone ringing from the Promise Keepers UK who said, 'No, no, we're not going to be like the American lot, we're really going to be such a group that you'll really be proud of us. And, in fact, unless we can feel that we've got people like you coming with us, we're not even sure that we want to go anywhere.' Now by the time you've written this up I don't know where it will be in terms of articulation.

But what's interesting is that they could even end up at point 4 if they did all their homework on the journey, and if they became a men's movement looking at the fundamental issues of masculinity in a post-feminist era. But I would have to be convinced that they'd got as far as that, because I don't think most of them have actually thought about women that much at all. I think they're just thinking about men.

So I think the answer to 'What place do men have in all this?' is that it has got to be a joint struggle. I'm convinced about that. But it's not that we're wanting men to join the women's struggle, our struggle. It's rather that we actually see that we're in this struggle together, men and women, for the same end, which is the Kingdom of God. We're at different places in the struggle but we're not asking the men to come on board and struggle for our sakes: it's also got to be their struggle, because there are issues for them to work out as well.

That's why Group 4 for me are in many ways the most attractive. It's wonderful to have men in Group 3 fighting with the women, but there are ways of doing that that are quite patronizing – 'we're here to help you, girls'. Whereas when it's their own articulation – trying to find languages of emotion, ways of expressing intimacy, even reformulations of liturgy – when it's their struggle as well, then I think the message has got home.

MARGARET: It's interesting to hear your line about the Promise Keepers, because the Catholic impression about the Promise Keepers is that this is not Group 1 but Group minus 1. That's to say that they seem to want to revert to an older view of society in which male and female roles were more sharply distinguished, with the woman the housewife and the man the breadwinner and decision-maker. But I don't think it's the sort of movement Catholics join, so maybe we're prejudiced.

But the other point of interest is the relationship between the Promise Keepers and the phenomenon of men's groups and men's spirituality, much of which I think is completely hilarious. But it does have a good side to it, or it can do, and I can see that men's spirituality groups could become eligible for position 4. So is it possible that you could get a confusion between Group 4 and Group minus 1?

ELAINE: No, I don't think so, I really don't think they can become confused. I think there's a lot of work to do before they can move from minus 1 to 4. That's why I need assurance when they say they're actually doing what the women are doing but they're doing it for themselves.

MARGARET: Is that what they say?

ELAINE: Well, that's how the issue is put to me, as something one can get on board. But then I have to be convinced. I said to this guy, 'You know we've done twelve years, fifteen years, twenty years of thinking about this. We've worked through loads of books, we've written our own books, we've thought about it, prayed about it, talked to one another. What have you done?' And the answer is, very little, in terms of thinking.

You can't shortcut the thinking time. You can shortcut it a bit, maybe you don't need fifteen years, but you do need a year or two, just to assimilate the literature and think yourself into a different mode. And I don't think they're there. But if the principle is there, if the heart is there, if the commitment really is to an egalitarian model with difference – where difference between the sexes is not barrier or boundary but just difference – and if the men are now trying to work out how best to be Christian men in a feminist Christian era, then I'm with it. But I'm not yet convinced that that's where it is.

MARGARET: It's interesting, isn't it, to note the meaning of single-sex groups...

ELAINE: Yes, that's right.

MARGARET: ...because an all-male group immediately makes women very suspicious, because we have the history of public schools and Oxbridge colleges and so on from which women were excluded.

ELAINE: And theological colleges and seminaries closed to women.

MARGARET: And so a men-only group meant, historically, power, exclusion, discrimination. Now we've got to the point where men-only groups and colleges have virtually been completely eradicated from our society, but we do have some women-only institutions. We have one college at Oxford which is still women-only – St Hilda's – and it's the women, particularly the students, who won't give that up. And they won't give it up for very feminist reasons: they want a kind of control over their lives, a sort of safe place without men coming in.

Of course, it's a very emotive area. I had a rather highly charged discussion – that's to say, I was the one who was emotional – with some friends recently about the habit of men dividing off for port at the end of a traditional dinner, which I find so offensive. The argument was, 'What's wrong with single-sex groups? We have male–male interaction and women–women interaction. It's nice for the women.'

So we're at this very interesting point in our history, when in terms of society's attribution of meaning, women-only groups are OK but men-only groups are not. So the very fact of

Promise Keepers being men-only raises suspicion. I suppose in due course the time will come when you can have men-only groups again.

Another group which you may know more about than I do, because it's more from your end of the church, is the Walk of a Thousand Men.

ELAINE: Yes, I know the chap who runs it, Daniel Cozens, he's a neighbour of ours in Cambridge. Yes, the Walk of a Thousand Men is actually quite similar to Promise Keepers in one way, in that the aim is to get men excited about their faith.

The argument is that men may well feel quite soppy about Christianity in front of women: where there are women and men together in churches, the men experience a spirituality vicariously through the women. That is the argument. The women are the ones who are doing the emotional stuff and the spiritual experience, and the men can often be getting it second hand, or else they're not articulating their faith nearly as well as the women do. So the way to nurture men to do this is to separate them from the women and let them find their own language of spirituality, their own language of communicating the gospel among each other.

Now to a certain extent that's partly what the Promise Keepers is about, too, but the Walk of a Thousand Men is distinctly an evangelization group. They do things that men like to do, which is the big outdoors, walking. They walk for days and days on end, stopping off at pubs anywhere they're walking, and communicating to all the other men in the pubs.

MARGARET: I used to have a beer mat for the Walk of a Thousand Men.

ELAINE: That's right, yes, they distribute those. Actually the chap whose brainchild it is is an evangelist, who over the years has seen many, many women come to a commitment to Christ and return to the church. And he has had a great longing to see men do the same.

So that's how it all started. How can we get men to respond for themselves and not just via their families, their kids, their wives? Well, we do it through men rather than just through women.

He's as sensitive as any to the title now, and every time I see him I get another explanation as to why the title's so important. I don't know whether there have ever been a thousand men on any particular walk, but I suppose if you add up all the men who have walked in a given year it would be a thousand plus.

MARGARET: How do you feel about that? Because there's still a bit of me that feels it's not fair, I'm not allowed to walk.

ELAINE: Yes, excluded. And women are there but they're not walking with the men.

MARGARET: They are supporting them, making their sandwiches, filling up their Thermos flasks.

ELAINE: Exactly.

MARGARET: And yet it must be true that it's very difficult for men. Of all the walks of life in which it is difficult for men, it must be most difficult in the church. And think how difficult it is for men even in secular society at the moment – the loss of a sense of identity and the constant barrage of feminist criticism. And in the churches, as you know, every group you ever go to is 95 per cent female. And what does that do to the men? It makes them feel as awful as it does when we go to a group that's 95 per cent men. So it is a problem, and one can see what good sense it makes to have a group just for men, but how do you do that without making me feel excluded?

ELAINE: I agree entirely. That is a big issue, and I think Danny is aware of that issue, too, and is facing the criticism all the time. But nevertheless the walks are still going on and still achieving great things.

They achieve multiple things. They achieve things, obviously, in terms of communication of the Christian gospel, but they also achieve an enormous amount with the people who go on the walk. It's not just male bonding, it's actually men walking together and reaching the next point – in other words, there's a goal. In doing that, they are starting to open up about themselves and share something of their own emotional life – their spiritual journey, their walk with God – and to raise issues that are still problematic for them, all in a context of safety. So there's an open vulnerability that exists there that you would probably never get in a church – because the time is limited to start with and there's so much business to get done in a set liturgy, and because there are women around and you let women do that kind of thing. But when you're walking for a whole day, with punctuation stops, then all kinds of stuff can come up.

I think in principle it's brilliant. I've had exactly the same reaction as you and felt very negative about it when Danny first started broadcasting it, but over the years I've thought, 'I trust this guy and I believe that he knows what he's doing.'

MARGARET: What you've just said opens up another question, and I really don't know what I think about this. You get

women in groups together 'sharing', that great 'in' word. Is it
or is it not good for men to put them in all-men groups so that
they can share too? From what you've just said it sounds
absolutely splendid and just what they need, but on the other
hand I know so many men who hate that sort of thing and
just feel that it's not a male thing to do. It embarrasses them,
it makes them squirm. They don't feel at all diminished by
not doing it, it's something women do, it's not what men do.
So to what extent should they be encouraged to bond
and share?

ELAINE: I'm sure that this group is a goal-orientated group,
it's an evangelistic group, so the main aim is communicating
the gospel, and the bonding comes as an aside. You've got a
shared pursuit, and it's a moment in life that people have giv-
en up time for, and therefore they make the most of it. It's a
time when people are given permission to be more human in
a whole range of ways, and they would be surprised at what
they have discovered. Daniel has never said, 'Look, this came
up and this came up,' because it's confidential to the group,
I suppose.

MARGARET: Maybe that's an important point, that you don't
label it as 'sharing' time...

ELAINE: No, that's right.

MARGARET: ...because that's what makes them squirm. I can
certainly think of conversations that Peter recounted, that
he'd had with male friends, when it was quite clear that something very intimate was being shared. It's what women would
call sharing, but they don't set out to do it, and maybe they're
quite rare occasions and for that they're even more valued.

ELAINE: There are also distinctly men's groups taking place in evangelicalism, a whole load of them. I don't know whether it was the first, but a significant one was set up by Roy McCloughry about ten years ago. He's an economist and sociologist, and he's been in the forefront of the gender debate and the growth of feminism, and he's a tremendous thinker. In the light of that he set up a men's group with, I think, eight people in it, and he wrote it up in his book, *Men and Masculinity* (Hodder & Stoughton, 1991).

His experience was interesting. They tried to find a common language that was non-competitive, and set demarcations for conversations and attitudes so they were not to compete with one another. They tried to find a language of emotion that they could share, a language of affirmation, but also exploration. The agenda was in an era where feminism had made men think again about masculinity.

There are some hilarious stories about the group. There are also some very poignant ones: over periods of years and years there was obviously a great deal of intimacy and sharing. Now these are not feely-touchy men – the ones I know of the group are what you'd call quite robust sorts of chaps, as Roy himself is – and yet they feel that they've accomplished something quite substantial.

MARGARET: I suppose what makes me feel this isn't quite where I am, is when they say, 'Let's explore what it means to be masculine.' I wouldn't feel happy being in a group of women that was saying, 'Let's explore what it means to be feminine.' Of course, I can explore what it means to be a woman in today's society, or to be a mother, or to be sexually female, but it's that 'feminine' or 'masculine' that raises the spectre of traditional roles for me.

ELAINE: In fact, the big criticism I've heard of Promise Keepers – this is the American Promise Keepers – is that it erects the ideology of masculinity, where masculinity and spirituality become almost co-terminous. Suddenly masculinity is back in, and spirituality is back in, but they're the same thing. And a 'real man' is Christ's man, and Christ is a phallic figure, and women are once again right on the edges, thinking 'Where are we in all of this?'

That's a big criticism of Promise Keepers. They probably haven't thought this thing through enough to realize what they're doing, but they've bitten into that whole genre that's been set down for them years before. We've been here before. So yes, I also feel a little bit uneasy about the question, 'What is my masculinity? What does it mean to be a masculine man?'

Thirteen

'DIFFERENCE'
AND THE EROTIC

ELAINE: For some a lesbian lifestyle seems to go hand in hand with feminist commitment. How can we explore this?

What strikes me is that, certainly from the seventies onwards, there has been a new coalition of feminist thinking. In the book I wrote some time ago, *What's Right with Feminism* (SPCK, 1985), I looked at three distinct and different types of feminism: liberal feminism, Marxist feminism and radical feminism. They each diagnose the issue differently.

The radical feminism was the most recent and the most vehement, but even that is now out of date. In revising my book, I included a new development, mostly from the late eighties: postmodern feminism. It incorporates a sexual critique, but also the critique of feminism itself by women of colour. And it feeds into Christian feminism in quite a powerful way.

What struck me is that the pivot of the debate is the concept of difference. At the very heart of it is the idea of trying to reclaim women's difference, without appealing to some form of essentialism.

In the 'pre-modern' period, it was assumed that differences were fixed, essential and located in biology. This lay behind the patriarchal structure of the church. Women were always in a subordinate position because of these God-given differences.

Women's differences were nearly always defined sexually by men: either women were men's temptresses, or (with the Victorian era) they were pure and angelic. But men and women were far apart.

Then the 'modern' phase of feminism was to eschew these differences and say we are really the same: both human. People defined this humanness in various ways: humanists claimed it was based in our rationality, Christians said it was in our common creation by God or our common membership of the body of Christ. But underlying them all was the idea of sameness and equality, which brings acceptance and partnership.

The postmoderns said that the idea of sameness is little better than the old ideology of separateness: women are still defined in relation to men, even if now they are seen as the same as men. For them, it is more important to retrieve the idea of difference, but to retrieve in a woman-defined way, which includes defining our own sexuality.

The focus on difference and sexuality brings together many of the post-Christian and postmodern thinkers. They all dissolve the so-called 'metanarratives' of the past.

MARGARET: What is a metanarrative?

ELAINE: Usually a metanarrative is seen as a big picture, a universal explanation of something. It's used a lot with regard to social or cultural issues. For example, Marxism offers a universal explanation: the history of society is the history of class struggles. Behaviourism relies on a metanarrative: all human behaviour develops in a stimulus–response environment. Liberation theology assumes a metanarrative: the Christian gospel is at heart about liberation from bondage and oppression. Although postmodernity has different nuances depending on whether we are talking about literature or architecture or social science, in general it is seen as turning its back on the metanarratives of modernity. It abandons universal concepts and goes for the particularity of experience and story.

The key postmodern feminist writers are French – Hélène Cixous, Julia Kristeva and Luce Irigaray – but even they are very different from each other. Much of their work hasn't been translated from French until recently, which is why it has been slow to penetrate the British–American scene. For years this 'school' was just called French feminism or psychoanalytic feminism – because of the interest in psychoanalysis (though it rebuffs much of Freud).

Anyway, postmodern feminism ultimately lets go of the universal concept of feminism and even of woman. And this process is aided by the critique of women of colour, who say that feminism has been a white, middle-class, western movement, and even in the church it has been developed by North American, British and Australian women in traditional, big, mainstream churches like the Catholic Church or the Episcopal Church. Their experience as women of colour is in very different cultures from this.

MARGARET: And so you get the black feminist movement that calls itself womanism.

ELAINE: Womanism probably first marked the splintering of the single feminist voice. It marked the demarcation away from a universal idea of woman's oppression. Womanist Christian writing challenges the idea that women experience the same kind of oppression within the church throughout different cultures and communities. The womanist voice says the struggles of black Christian feminists within the church are very different from those of white Christian feminists. There are different layers and areas of oppression, and 'white' concepts of liberation are inadequate. As Audre Lourde insisted, 'We can't use the master's tools to dismantle the master's house.'

A woman leader of a black-led church once pointed out to me that the way we use colour imagery in Christian language and symbolism is to equate 'black' or 'dark' with evil, or sin, or something sinister. She said that even though people have become sensitized to gender bias in language it is still difficult to get them to take colour bias seriously. She finds it painful to be accused of simply nit-picking. To object, when a word used to describe her appearance is used elsewhere always in a pejorative sense, is not a matter of picking nits.

MARGARET: One of the most difficult words to get racially right is 'blackmail', but Desmond Tutu, I noticed, used the alternative: 'whitemail'. At least you know what he means, otherwise I don't know what you do with that one. These things do matter enormously.

I agree the traditional language is very racist, with white angels and black devils, and that is deeply ingrained in us. It does need new concepts. We must become aware of this and aware of when we are operating as a liberator on one front and an oppressor on another.

ELAINE: We must also include the plurality of other women's voices, for example the Maori, Samoan or Fiji feminists and women from most of the Pacific Islands. Maori artist Roman Potiki, who works also in drama, writes about the indigenous Maori women's exploration of identity. For them, theatre has become a key way of debunking myths and raising central questions like: 'Who am I? Where do I come from? Where do I belong?' And their answers are different from those of Pakeha women (white New Zealanders).

MARGARET: Also linked is the mujerista movement. Have you heard of that?

ELAINE: No, I don't know about that.

MARGARET: Something I've heard of that you haven't – how rare! This is the Hispanic counterpart to the Afro-American 'womanist', because *mujer* is the Spanish for 'woman'. I first heard the term used by that bright young Argentinian woman theologian at Edinburgh University, Marcella Althaus-Reid, but there are a number of Hispanic theologians in the States who call themselves by that name. Possibly their focus is more on linking together women and poverty, with a more direct link to liberation theology, whereas the womanists link together women and race.

ELAINE: There are two things I want to say here. One is that the globalization of poverty is largely focused on women and their children. There is a justified allegation that while women in the north are fighting for equal access, there are blind spots about the way women in the third world are oppressed by the culture of consumerism and end up working all hours for a pittance so that we can enjoy affluent lives. Somehow, even as Christian women, we can cut that out and not see it as part of our task to bring real liberation to our sisters. It's not surprising that articulate women become very angry about this. I was delighted to be asked to be President of Tear Fund because we take issues of both gender and economic oppression seriously.

The second thing is the way we talk about black men. White women may offer a critique of white male attitudes, but black women sometimes tell me they feel alienated when they hear black men being scapegoated as the enemy.

With the development, then, of different versions of feminism in different cultures, everybody is wanting to define their own response to oppression. So there is a massive fragmentation, and the concept of difference becomes doubly important because it signifies not only difference between men and women, but difference between women and women.

The fundamental question underlying this is: 'Can women share their experiences of God, of spirituality and the church?' And the response seems to be 'No, not really, because there isn't a universal experience to share.' Sisterhood is based on a myth, for we all have our own different experiences and interpretations, which often clash with each other. There are oppressions within the women's camp as well as between women in the big thing called patriarchy.

MARGARET: So does it mean that the word 'sisterhood' is now out of fashion?

ELAINE: In a global sense, yes, in that it was a white, middle-class word imposed on women of other cultures, inviting them to take on a white woman's agenda in a way that often masked or falsely nuanced their own oppression.

MARGARET: That's very helpful, because I have heard bits and pieces of this postmodern feminism in lectures, and I have never quite understood it. I first heard about Irigaray at one of the meetings of the European Society of Women in Theological Research, in Bristol in 1991. There was an entire workshop on this woman. And all the Brits said, 'How very odd,' for nobody had heard of her. Since then people have heard about her more and more, but never actually read her. And now I have heard her name so often that I can even pronounce it.

ELAINE: I came to it the other way round, because I heard post-Christian women talking about how we must move towards the erotic, away from *agape* love, which they see as male and bodiless and dispassionate. *Eros* takes us back to women's earth-bodily connectedness, and emphasizes that human beings are people of flesh as well as of spirit. We can only understand women's difference when we relinquish *agape* and move towards the erotic. It was the Korean theologian...

MARGARET: The one with the fire, who invoked the spirit of earth, air and water at the World Council of Churches meeting in Canberra in 1988, Chung Hyun Kyung?

ELAINE: That's the one. And Carter Heyward in the States. But it was not until I started to read the French writers that I realized that the reclaiming of the erotic comes from them, and these feminists within the church have borrowed the idea. Irigaray talks about *jouissance*, by which she means uninhibited female sensuality, the awareness of our own bodiliness and the enjoyment of the fact that we are duality, spirit and flesh. We are connected and relational, men are unitary and single. But this *jouissance* is very similar to the 'erotic' as used by Chung and Heyward, except Heyward identifies it more definitely as a spiritual force, linked with the power that she calls Christa (Carter Heyward, *Touching Our Strength*, HarperCollins, 1989, pp. 85–118).

MARGARET: You mean Christa the female, crucified Christ?

ELAINE: Yes and no. Christa is not just a female Christ, a woman on the cross. Christa is spirit-power, woman-power, God-power and *eros*-power. Christa is not an incarnate or reified being, but a force moving between women, a divine love which is women. The Christian idea that God is outside us, overwhelming us with love, is replaced with the notion that we are overwhelmed by love within us. Love, *eros*, Christa is to do with our internal and relational lives, with our bodies and our choices as women. For me, this is the link with the notion of *jouissance* in the French feminists.

MARGARET: And Christa used in this sense, is this used by Christians?

ELAINE: It is difficult to say whether Carter Heyward is Christian or post-Christian.

MARGARET: She calls herself Christian.

ELAINE: Yes, in that she is a priest in the Anglican Church.

MARGARET: Then I would call her a Christian.

ELAINE: But her Christianity is very different from everyone else's. Maybe this wasn't a good topic to choose.

MARGARET: No, this was a very good topic because it is something I don't understand, and it's very new.

ELAINE: I have been reading so much of the postmodern feminists for the last two months really. I should have a book with me because I carry one around. How about that? Look.

MARGARET: *Engaging with Irigaray* edited by Caroline Burke, Naomi Shaw, Margaret Whitford, in the series *Feminist*

Philosophy and Modern European Thought (Columbia, 1996).
Gosh. Rather hard work.

ELAINE: It is heavy going. It has transformed my journeys on
the Underground.

MARGARET: I don't think I understand this very well, so let
me try and say it back to you.

We start with the old patriarchal thing – the caricature of
men and women. Men and women are essentially different
and all that.

Incidentally, that old view of difference is rather like a
hilarious thing I saw on Harry Enfield's show. It was an early
twentieth-century dinner party, shot in black and white, all
going in a very jolly way. Then suddenly the men start talking
about the gold standard and a woman puts forward an opinion, a very intelligent opinion. Everyone freezes, it is dead
embarrassing, and the husband stands up and takes the
woman straight home. You see, the woman should have said,
'I don't know much about the gold standard but I do love little kittens, they are so soft and furry.'

Then there were diagrams. Look what happens when
information gets into a male brain: it fills up consistently.
Now look at the same diagram with a woman's brain: at first it
looks as though the same thing is happening, but suddenly
it can't take any more. You get squirly scribbles all over the
brain. The woman has suffered information overload and she
gets confused.

That is the old essentialism.

Then you get modern feminism, which stresses sameness,
equality and the rights of women. Having got away from the
old caricatures of women defined by sexuality – virgin, wife,
mother, whore – you get the attempt by women to play an

equal role in society, which I feel very much involved in, actually.

But now this new postmodern approach coming out of France is saying: we want to bring sexuality back in, but not in the old way, not as woman seen as a sexual being through male eyes, but I myself, rediscovering my body. So I as a woman become the actor, and experience whatever erotic feelings I may feel, whether towards a man or a woman.

ELAINE: Yes, that's right. And I explore the seat of my erotic feelings. Like Germaine Greer, but with a different focus, Irigaray has a whole lot on women's anatomy – on the vulva particularly (Irigaray, *This Sex which is not One*, Cornell University Press, 1985). She focuses on the fact that women have multiple erogenous zones, unlike the man, who has just got a penis.

Therefore this whole multiple, experiential, psycho-sexual, emotional base that women have means that we are much more complex. We have many, many seats to our eroticism. And she links that to the complexity of women's emotional and experiential responses to life in general.

MARGARET: I am a little unclear about how the notion of difference leads on to the notion of the erotic.

ELAINE: Simone de Beauvoir is the link. She was very much inside Marxism and liberation theory, and she starts this whole French tradition. Her argument was always that man was Self with a capital S and woman was Other with a capital O – she didn't argue for that, she argued against it. Women live under this kind of this dichotomy, this stereotype, and we have to know how to deal with it.

MARGARET: It is written into the very language. 'Man' means man and woman, 'he' means he and she.

ELAINE: So now the French feminists say Simone de Beauvoir was right. But let's use that difference. If man is Self and woman is Other, let's be Other. Let's embrace our difference, our erotic sensuality, not as the old female 'essence' but as a way of combating patriarchy, or what Irigaray calls 'phallocentrism'.

A word on postmodernism. It used to be the case that we had names for theories or positions which emerged from the writings of a particular person or group, so we called people Marxists or Freudians or whatever. But now you are always post-something. So Kristeva, for example, is a post-Freudian psychoanalytic thinker. The whole idea of being postmodern or post-Christian is that you are defining yourself in terms of what comes after, but what comes after is a mystery. We don't know what comes after Christianity, we don't know what comes after modernity, so all we can do is call it 'post'.

I think even the word 'post' is an admission of defeat. It is a sort of nihilistic response: we don't know what this is but it is just something that came after.

MARGARET: And there is a post-Marxist thing as well, didn't you say?

ELAINE: Yes, in a certain sense I think almost all feminists after Marxist feminism are post-Marxist in some way, even the postmoderns. The French were around at the disturbances in Paris in May 1968. They set up then this group called *Psychanalyse et Politique*, linking psychoanalysis and politics together. So right from the beginning you had this idea that political awareness also involves our internal, emotional analysis. Again it stems back to a Marxist period in French radical history and popular movements in the 1960s, the same thing really that spearheaded the radical feminists in the States, but it took a different form in France, that was all.

I am probably boring you to tears.

MARGARET: No, it's not that. It's just that I have heard these ideas quite a lot and they have never settled with me. I have never understood what difference they would make to my faith or to the way I live my life. Can you throw any light on why I hear these ideas, and they flow over me? Obviously they are making an impression on other people, aren't they?

ELAINE: They are gripping a lot of people. But they flow over me, too. I have had to struggle to read the stuff, and to get inside it. I had some time to do it on sabbatical, otherwise I would never have done it.

At the end of the day I think it flows over us because their starting point is wrong! I don't think life is fundamentally about women's difference nor about *jouissance* and the erotic.

MARGARET: How does the lesbian thing come in? Is it that if sexuality is defined by women themselves, and they are no longer a sex object in one way or another for men, then that frees them to choose? If it depends on choice it would seem to free them not only for lesbianism but also for bestiality or auto-eroticism, as well as heterosexuality.

ELAINE: There is a lot of auto-eroticism in it. I think that is almost encouraged as an authentic response to one's own body. Bestiality I have never come across in any of the writings, I don't think that is encouraged. I think the problem with heterosexuality for most of them is that it is too tied in with the old essentialism and a patriarchal agenda. The moment you step back into a heterosexual relationship you are buying into patriarchal definitions of your sexuality.

So many of them do see a lesbian expression of the erotic or *jouissance*, because it is seen as something that women can only fully explore with other women. Our *jouissance* seems to be most fully articulated when we are sharing it with other people for whom *jouissance* is also possible, rather than being limited by this unitary idea of the male penis. Carter Heyward argues something very similar. She defines and describes the erotic nearly always in terms of women loving women. She doesn't discount heterosexuality, but I haven't come across any reference to men in erotic Christa-powered relations. She is talking about women loving women.

MARGARET: But aren't they affected in any way by the fact that the human race has continued through heterosexual sex?

ELAINE: That doesn't seem to have formed a very big part of their argument. They are more interested in one's experience of love as a woman.

MARGARET: Do they say anything about motherhood?

ELAINE: There is a lot of approbation of motherhood, but not motherhood within patriarchy. It is a kind of chosen motherhood: motherhood as giving oneself to others through choice. Motherhood is part of the erotic life of women, in terms of enjoying the physical. But then, if you are to ask where the children come from, that's a question that is not raised. The fact that you need male sperm is often convenient-ly ignored.

MARGARET: And no mention of the fact that a father around the place could sometimes make some kind of contribution?

ELAINE: I don't think they deny that, it's just not the focus of their writings. They are really only interested in talking to and about women.

MARGARET: So that is different from modern feminism, because the modern feminist – I suppose I am one – would say the father ought to be changing nappies too, and cooking meals. But these postmodern feminists just want to explore what it means to be a woman?

ELAINE: Yes, and they refer to it as a woman-identified framework or as a woman-centred framework.

MARGARET: And this is what the John Redwoods of this world so detest. Because it leads to single parenthood, not as an accident or as a misfortune, but as an ideal.

ELAINE: Probably. But it is a kind of writing that doesn't talk any more about ideals.

MARGARET: What happens when we ask how this can help or hinder Christian feminism? There is the one example of Carter Heyward, who makes her own synthesis with the idea of the Christa, but we both feel profoundly unconvinced.

ELAINE: And uncomfortable with it. Particularly when her image of erotic love between women becomes identified with the Eucharist.

MARGARET: I have never heard that before.

ELAINE: In her chapter on 'The erotic as power', which I mentioned earlier, she has a powerful passage on her delight at celebrating the body of Christa 'as eternal resource of nourishment on the sacred journey towards justice'. Then she goes on to describe something like lesbian lovemaking with Christa as its ground and power. She says, 'I take her and stroke her playfully. I look upon her with immense tenderness. I take her and nibble a little. I take her and eat, take her and drink. I am taken, grasped and caressed by her power moving between us. Immersing myself in you, with you, through you, I move with you in the sensual wellspring of her love ... in the turbulence of her passion.'

Heyward deliberately uses Eucharistic language because this is the Eucharist for her. The Eucharist is the sacrifice of love, not of a God out there, or a Christ out there, or a life out there or a church out there. It is love in here, love as experienced through women.

Certainly, she believes there are social ramifications in terms of justice and working for the oppressed. But epistemologically it is all about internal and relational love between women. The idea of a transcendent God is completely absent, left behind as a myth, which has kept women in chains.

MARGARET: I haven't read this stuff but let me attempt a defence. Carter Heyward did the Holy Week sermons at St James's Piccadilly one year and my mother, who is a very traditional Anglican, went. She liked her. She didn't know anything about her, but this was someone who could preach helpfully.

ELAINE: She can, yes, and when you hear her on the biblical texts it can be quite moving. But when you ask her what she means by it, at a philosophical and a fundamental theological level, I think she is a million miles away.

MARGARET: One is uncomfortable, isn't one, with the promotion of lesbianism? Where is it in the States that had such a reputation for lesbianism that it was almost impossible to go and study theology there?

ELAINE: That is probably her place. She used to be at the Episcopal Divinity School in Cambridge, Massachusetts.

MARGARET: A Canadian friend of mine went to a conference there, and she said it was really embarrassing, although she is a feminist theologian herself. People were sitting in couples all over the floor, lolling against each other. Then everyone was asked to declare their sexuality, and if you happened to say you were heterosexual you felt very small. And if you said you didn't wish to disclose, you were made to feel even smaller. There was a sense that you weren't a proper sister unless you loved women. But that is using the language of sisterhood, which you say is going out.

ELAINE: Yes, although, of course, for some it stays important. But I have problems with what you describe, and especially with a lesbian agenda within the church. I have thought a good deal about the gay and lesbian celebration at Southwark Cathedral. Is this something to be celebrated or not?

Our response to God is always to be celebrated if it is a response of love and humility and asking for God's forgiveness and wholeness. If that was what was being celebrated, then that is wonderful. But if what was being celebrated is our autonomous sexuality and our right to define our own sexual lives, I have problems with that. If what was being celebrated was that the church gives us no guidance on our options but leaves it all to us, then I think that was wrong. There is a much biblical teaching on sexual love and behaviour which is very relevant today.

MARGARET: Now that is interesting. I wasn't at Southwark but I very much wanted to be there. It happened to be the one week I could book in for a retreat, but I sent them a financial contribution and made it clear I would be very much there in spirit.

Now, what am I saying in giving them that support? I am saying that I think the church has marginalized homosexuals appallingly throughout its history, and that as a heterosexual woman I want to stand by them. I am saying that there is too simplistic a transfer to the present day of what is supposed to be biblical sexual morality. I am saying that I recognize that there are Christian homosexuals whose personal experience is that their sexuality does not lead them away from God but towards God. I am saying that I welcome the exploration of these issues, against very intense opposition, by the Lesbian and Gay Christian Movement. And I am saying that I reject any attempt to drive a wedge through their psyche and make them choose between one part of their being that is necessary for their fulfilment and another part of their being that is necessary for their fulfilment.

ELAINE: I can't get away from the meaning of sexuality as an expression of the bi-unity of the human race. In the Genesis narrative, God does not go back to create a woman, as another separate creation, but takes the one human being and makes it into two. Sexual union is where, in biblical language, we become 'one flesh' again. That implies that male and female together represent wholeness and unity. Of course, unity doesn't necessarily have to be sexual. It means that partnership is what we are always striving towards: partnership, mutual respect, recognition and togetherness, not hierarchy or inequality, nor absolute difference. It is the unity of humanness expressed as the image of God.

Now where homosexuality fits into that I don't know, and so I have to see it as something that deviates from the central norm. But then so do many other things in our lives deviate. So the bigger issue for me is a pastoral one rather than a theological one. How do we relate to people who do not 'fit' our theology of sexuality? And I think my response is that I should just love them. We must try and work with people who are in that position, help them to be faithful to God and seek the best for them, rather than heaping judgement and finding ways of making their lives a misery.

MARGARET: The problem about seeing homosexuality as deviant is that it doesn't seem to be the personal experience of people who are homosexuals. I can't speak for this because I haven't had that experience, but their experience, and there are very good Christians among them, so often seems to be that this is how God has made them.

Fourteen

ABORTION

MARGARET: This is the one issue where I part company with most feminists, which is sad. They feel I am not sufficiently on the side of women, but being on the side of women should not lead to oppression of another group. And if the foetus is a human baby – that's a big 'if', but if it is – then there's no way one can put the rights of the woman first, to the point of killing that human being. That's completely straightforward.

I take a very primitivist approach to whether it is a baby. If it looks like a baby, I think it is. If it doesn't, I'd say I'm agnostic about it.

ELAINE: When you say, 'If it doesn't', do you mean because it's in an embryonic state?

MARGARET: If it looks like a blob of jelly.

Then there is an earlier state when I'm pretty certain it's not a baby. This would separate me from the other side, the pro-lifers who are absolutely adamant that from the moment of conception this is a human being. My problem with that is that, up to the time of twinning, it seems logically and philosophically impossible that it can be a human being, because you can't have a human being dividing into two human beings. I've even heard an absurd theory that in twinning you have one half parenting the other, a parent embryo and a child embryo. That seems to me nonsense, because that is not how human beings reproduce themselves. And there are so many natural miscarriages at the very, very early stage that I can't find it in myself to be overconcerned.

So although I would think it better not to interfere at all, nonetheless the consequences of pregnancy are so enormous – as I fully know, having had three children – that I would not actually object to anyone using the coil, or taking the morning-after pill, to stop a pregnancy before the period of potential twinning is over, which is around a week, I think.

Then you have a grey area from the missed period up to a point of clarity when it has got arms and legs and eyes and ears and fingers and toes and when you stick a pin in, it reacts with pain. So I'm less unhappy about early abortions than about late ones, because there is an element of doubt in my mind. But the law we have, allowing abortion up to birth in the case of handicap – that has got to be wrong.

Did you see any of those Channel 4 programmes recently, in a week of programmes on abortion?

ELAINE: No, when was this?

MARGARET: To mark the thirtieth anniversary of the Abortion Act. Those programmes were useful contributions to the debate, because they didn't come from any one lobby. In a society which generally is pro-choice I thought it was quite an advance to be open-minded and interview people about how they felt about their abortions.

One particular late-night discussion called *After Dark* (1 November 1997) went on for about three and a half hours, and had me absolutely fascinated. There was a moral philosopher on it...

ELAINE: Do you remember who it was?

MARGARET: Professor John Harris of Manchester.

ELAINE: Yes, I know who you mean.

MARGARET: ...and he was cornered, about three hours into the discussion, into saying – and he said it without resistance, a good conscientious academic – that there was no moral difference between killing a child before birth and killing a child after birth, up to the age of about eighteen months. At that point for me the argument was over.

ELAINE: It was lost. Absolutely.

MARGARET: Now I also saw the Pro-life Alliance party political broadcast which was censored. In fact I organized for *The Tablet* a whole page of reactions to it.

It was gutting. I went to the press showing, which was full of brash young women reporters – I work in this world, I know how pushy they are – and they were told before it started, 'If you want to look away, look away.' I was sitting in the front row, and while it was showing I turned round and saw several looking away. These would be the kind of women who fight for the right to choose, and when it came to looking at what they were fighting for they felt sick and couldn't take it.

Elaine, you can't believe it, it was awful. We saw skulls smashed up. And the fact that they were so soft made it even worse.

ELAINE: More poignant, yes.

MARGARET: And little legs and arms. We are ignoring what we are doing because we don't see it. I know as well as anyone how having a baby completely disrupts the whole of your life. But you can't go around killing other people because of that.

ELAINE: Exactly.

MARGARET: And do you remember that woman, Caroline Beale? She had a baby in her hotel room when she was on holiday in the United States, and killed it immediately it was born – whether by mistake or not was unclear. The reaction in the States was horror: 'How could any mother murder her child? She must be so unnatural.' Yet seconds earlier that would have been OK according to the logic of the abortion lobby. It doesn't make sense. It's a question of what you see, and the campaign to stop people seeing it is wrong.

ELAINE: There have been a lot of dogmas and theological debates in the past that have missed the point: natural law, for example. I think the real issues concentrate round the meaning of human personhood. For me the fundamental question is not, 'Is this child a person and should we do this to persons?' Children, either alive or *in utero*, are persons and we should not kill them, full stop. The real debate is more, 'When is a person?'

I remember discussing this with John Habgood when he was Archbishop of York. I found to my delight that we shared the same concern but probably put the 'when' at different points. I understood his view to be that once we establish that there is a person, at whatever stage that is, then that person is entitled to total personal dignity. There are things that you may not do to persons, whatever your circumstances. My position is the same, with more emphasis. No matter how inconvenient it is, no matter how it is going to affect our lives or change the future from now on, we cannot do it, we cannot kill people.

MARGARET: One laughs, but one should cry.

ELAINE: I know, but it's as ridiculous as that, isn't it? So why is it that people can't see it?

I've worked through this with quite a few feminists over the years, particularly young women from universities. When I first wrote a book on feminism I got a barrage of complaints from women who were upset about me taking what they saw as an anti-abortion, anti-woman line. In discussion with them it was evident that they did not see a foetus as an autonomous human being, separate from its mother's cell structure. Therefore, being part of a woman's cell structure, she had the right to say what she wanted to happen to her own body.

The abortion rights campaign was part of women's growing into autonomy. They wanted the right to make their own decisions about their own bodies rather than be subject to decisions by either medics or the church. Now I agree that women are entitled to a greater degree of autonomy in many areas, but where these feminists and I differ fundamentally is that I don't think this is one of those areas. For a human foetus is not simply my cell structure. (S)he is a separate person, a lodger, someone else, not me.

It was always a frustrating discussion and they would simply say, 'We cannot believe that,' but it was almost saying, 'We will not believe that, we will not believe that this is a person, because once we do we've lost the argument.' Most women needed to think of a foetus as a part of their own body because it was neater that way. One woman conceded that if it could be proved that a foetus could feel pain or fear or anxiety she would change her views. But when pretty conclusive evidence was produced it made no difference. It was just interpreted as anti-abortion rhetoric.

I suppose most feminists divide into two groups: the ones who frankly don't care and are pretty hardened about the whole thing, and the others who may feel compassion towards vulnerable beings but who also believe that the self-identified needs of a woman should be allowed to come first.

MARGARET: You focused on the question of 'When is a person?' Let's look at that. I tend not to use that language because it's so difficult to find a definition of a person that would include the newborn babe and also someone brain-damaged in PVS (permanent vegetative state). So how would you define a person?

ELAINE: I used to spend hours of lecturing time trying to define a person. We have been deeply affected in the west by the Enlightenment definition that a person is an autonomous, rational individual. That has gripped our culture for a couple of hundred years. Personal identity was seen in terms of our separateness, difference, individuation, and later in terms of self-consciousness or awareness.

In the late twentieth century this focus has opened the door to all kinds of distortions and abuses. Peter Singer argues, for example, that not all human life is equal. He divides people into those who are real persons and those who are non-persons or not-quite persons, and who therefore should not be afforded the same dignity. So consciousness, self-awareness, ability to make your own choices, ability to enter into interactive relationships, the experience of pleasure, are all very central to his understanding of the person, because he puts so much emphasis on personal autonomy.

Our problem in the west is that we've taken too much notice of the Enlightenment. If we'd taken more notice of the Christian tradition we would be working with a very different concept of the person now. In Christian theology, persons are defined relationally. We are persons because we are created in the image of God – in relationship with the Creator. My personhood resides in the fact that I am created by God, dependent, creaturely, not autonomous, and responsive to God. Because we are relational we are communal, not individualistic: we are members of one another.

So that shifts the whole focus. All persons are persons, whether they think or not, whether they are in PVS or not, whether they are minus arms and legs or not, because there is something in their very created nature that is relational to God who made them. And it's in that relationship that personhood resides.

MARGARET: Two questions on that. About Peter Singer: what sort of persons would he place in his second-class category?

ELAINE: Oh, loads. Those lacking capacity for self-awareness, genetically defective infants. He attacks what he calls speciesism, which discriminates in favour of human beings over other species of life. He says, for example: 'The more intellectually sophisticated non-human animals have a mental and emotional life that in every significant respect equals or surpasses that of the most profoundly intellectually disabled human beings.' And here's another bit: 'There is no reason to think that a fish suffers less when dying in a net than a foetus suffers during an abortion, hence the argument for not eating fish is much stronger than the argument against abortion' (*Rethinking Life and Death*, Macmillan, 1994).

MARGARET: Oh God, does he really say that?

ELAINE: Yes. In fact we have a moral duty to abortion or even infanticide when the child is seriously genetically defective. His universe seems to be constructed around consciousness and rationality and ability to make autonomous choices.

MARGARET: Well, I'm very glad that I have so often insisted that I'm a speciesist. Which I only do to annoy other theologians. There you are, you see, that's the logic of it.

ELAINE: Singer seems to mount a consistent attack on the Christian position – that all human life is of equal value and dignified before God. His alternative is stark, for if you fall on the wrong side it seems you may justifiably be annihilated.

I find, though, that other people as well as Christians don't want to live in Singer's universe. Many of them think it is horrendous and insist, 'No, I don't want to go down that route. What stops me? Where are the alternatives? Is there another avenue?'

MARGARET: And that points them towards Christianity sometimes?

ELAINE: Yes, even if they don't want to take on board the whole Christian system, they want a cut-off point much earlier than Singer. John Wyatt, a neonatal specialist and professor at Queen Mary Hospital, has a brilliant Christian critique of Singer in *Matters of Life and Death*. He says many people have a gut reaction against him and want a rationale for avoiding his conclusions. Being in dialogue with people who see where his arguments lead makes Christians realize we have far more friends than we thought.

MARGARET: My second question is about the relational definition: I'm not sure how satisfying I find that. In terms of our
relationship with our Creator, what makes the relationship of
a foetus to the Creator superior to the relationship of a mon-
key to the Creator?

Because of this difficulty in drawing the line about when
someone becomes a person, I have reverted to – perhaps never
left – the old and highly unfashionable language of the soul.
I know that is now really looked down on, but it seems to me
to do the job required.

Of course, I don't think the soul is a sort of invisible thing
that flies into the air when we die. I don't think anyone ever
did think that, actually. It is a way of saying that human rights
should be accorded no matter how damaged someone is, on
the one hand, at the end of life, or how much a matter of
potentiality, at the beginning of life. And human rights are
not negotiable, they do not come because we choose to give
them, they are absolute.

Although I've talked about the grey area of early abortions,
philosophically it doesn't make sense to have a gradualist
view about this. You either have human rights or you don't.
You don't gain them bit by bit, just as at the end of life you
don't lose them bit by bit, or else it would be all right to do
away with your old granny with Alzheimer's. How do you protect the old granny? You have to say that whether she's black,
white, able, disabled, conscious or unconscious, she has
human rights.

The question then is, 'When do you get them?' and I'm
not quite sure at what early stage of human development that
is. But I'm sure there must be a stage, it's just that we don't
have enough scientific knowledge – perhaps we never will – to
know when it is. One can find a point when clearly those
rights must be there, and another point when really you can't

see that they possibly could be there. It's another way of talking about 'When is there a human being?'

ELAINE: Yes. I've been into personhood for a long time! Teaching philosophy over a number of years engages you in questions like 'Is the soul a substance?' and 'What's the relationship between the soul and the self?'

MARGARET: Do you believe in the soul?

ELAINE: Um...

MARGARET: No.

ELAINE: Well, if we want to call that kernel of our personhood the soul or self, fine. I don't mind what we call it. I recognize a human being when I see one.

MARGARET: That's it. 'I recognize a human being when I see one.' That's the problem with the unborn child, we don't see it.

ELAINE: I suppose you're right.

I find it interesting to talk to people doing embryonic research. I remember one man, who fertilizes human eggs in test tubes, saying that he's quite happy to put the fertilized egg down the sluice, because in a test tube or dish it won't grow into a person. It is just an experimental process, not an issue of human dignity.

But I was talking to another doctor recently who said when he fertilizes an egg out of the womb it is always with the idea of implanting it. Therefore the moment the egg is fertilized he accords it dignity. He says a fertilized embryo in the right place becomes a person. So he is much happier when it's back in the womb, because then if nothing else stops it a person will be born.

The beginning area is grey for me as long as there is uncertainty that this whatever-we-have-here is a significant human life. But the moment it is, and I would give it the benefit of the doubt earlier rather than later, then the mist clears. From then onwards, to terminate life is wrong. Certainly by the time the heart is beating, there isn't any more doubt about it.

MARGARET: I'm really glad to find we agree on this, because when I suggested the topic I didn't know what your views were. But it occurred to me that this is one of the feminist issues that there is something to say about, in Christian terms.

ELAINE: Should we turn to the question about how we help women struggling in this area? We have to acknowledge that in instances of abuse, incest or rape, abortion is some women's way of trying to put the violence behind them and start life afresh. I personally came across a case like that, some years ago. I met a woman, completely by accident, who had suffered a vicious rape, and I suggested she went straight to the doctor to sort it out. It seemed important to have it dealt with straight away, whatever it was, but she didn't want to go because it meant going to the police first.

MARGARET: You met her by chance?

ELAINE: Yes, she was totally distraught in a public loo. I didn't know anything about her, but I believed her story. A friend had just found her in a state of numbed shock. Anyway, we all talked for some time, and the friend took her off to the police station, and then on to the hospital, as far as I know. Apparently they both knew the guy quite well, and there were all kinds of reasons for her not wanting to go public on it. But on the other hand she kept saying, 'If this turns into a baby I couldn't ever see it through.'

MARGARET: I think that's exactly right, because she would be going so early. It just would not be an abortion.

ELAINE: It makes it easier when neither she nor the hospital would even know whether any conception had taken place. I didn't have any qualms at all.

MARGARET: Why did she have to go to the police before the doctor? Is it because they have to take tests for DNA evidence, in case any charges are brought?

ELAINE: Something like that. I think now that a police-woman accompanies a woman to the hospital and sees it through with her. In the case of an attack, the hospital would have to call the police anyway.

These cases are straightforward. But what about women who don't want the baby for other reasons? Perhaps they are not healthy, or the marriage is packing in, or they have too many children, or all of those at once. What is the Christian response here?

One woman I was helping was in this situation. In a diffi-cult marriage they had probably had one night of sex in about two years, and she became pregnant. She already had four children, she was profoundly depressed and she wanted me to say, 'Go ahead and have this abortion, it's obviously the right thing.' I couldn't. She knew I couldn't. Even though I wanted the best for her, I couldn't say that.

She went to the abortion clinic, ten weeks into the pregnancy rather than six, and even then found it hard to go through with. Afterwards, she cried and screamed and wanted the baby back. It was really awful for her. She had phoned me the night before and asked if she should have the abortion. I said, 'I can't make that decision for you. You know what I believe about abortion. I also think it's wrong for you, but I can't make your decision.' I thought I was giving her autonomy, because so many people had taken it from her in the past. But I wondered afterwards if I should just have said, 'Don't do it.'

Afterwards, it really affected her husband. He had been pressurizing her into a termination but when he saw what it had done to her he was devastated. It changed his attitude towards her. They both had to come to terms with guilt, but it marked a turning point. She felt she had to ask forgiveness from the baby. She wasn't a church attender, but she wanted some prayers for the baby and to give it a name. I think it was a real healing process. It was wonderful.

She did become pregnant again. Their marriage is much stronger now, even with five children! She wanted to have another baby, to show this first baby, the one that she had destroyed...

MARGARET: ...that she was sorry.

ELAINE: That's right.

MARGARET: I know of a case of a girl who was adopted – so she is aware that she owes her life to the fact that her mother didn't do this – and she got pregnant. She agonized, and went into it in great detail, and decided that she could not have an abortion after the foetus had reached a certain stage of development – I think it was eight weeks. She went private because the National Health would make her wait another two weeks. It was to some extent with a divided conscience.

But I do respect it, because I think that is the right principle. And her way of compensating for the life she had taken – I don't think she thinks it was wrong, but she is nonetheless uneasy – was to become an egg donor. That is actually something I am not very happy about, but I can see what it means to her that she doesn't want to be taking away a life.

I don't think there are any easy answers. I would reject utterly the answer that, 'You took the risk, you had sex, so you must live with the consequences.' It could happen to any of us. At the very least, with rape it could happen to any of us. But the whole area of sexuality and sexual behaviour is so difficult, always. As Jesus said to those who were going to stone the adulterous woman, 'Let the one who is without sin throw the first stone' (John 8:7).

So I don't think that is the answer, and I don't think the answer is to say you can always have the baby adopted. I don't think that is an option nowadays in the way it used to be.

ELAINE: No, it's a shame that it's not.

MARGARET: How could you live with the thought that eighteen years along the line your child might come back to you and say, 'Why did you give me away?' There was a time when you could answer, 'I was really advised it was for the best. I knew that you would be so discriminated against as an illegitimate child that I decided to give you a better life. It broke my heart to do it, and I've been in agony over it ever since. But it was out of love for you that I did it.' That used to be true. It's not true any more.

ELAINE: At the same time it's an enormous act of love for a woman to bring a baby to full term and have it adopted. It's probably a bigger act of love than ever before, because there are so many pressures to having the baby destroyed. It's a lot to ask of a woman, to carry a baby for nine months and then give it up.

MARGARET: And to go through the birth process.

ELAINE: Precisely. If one could do that, I think it would be an incredibly loving act, a deeply loving, sacrificial act.

MARGARET: Well, that's the other side of it.

ELAINE: It was Germaine Greer, wasn't it, who suggested that couples ought to adopt the pregnant girl and baby as a unit? Then the girl, having brought the child into the world, would know the parents who were taking this on, and would be free to come and go and visit, and to stay in touch with the child as long as she wanted to.

MARGARET: And she could go off and do her studies or whatever she wanted to do with her life. And she would have childcare provided, that was not just impersonal but actually an adoptive mother.

ELAINE: That's right, yes.

MARGARET: That's a beautiful idea. I'm sure that suggestion is on the right lines.

But one of the interesting statistics is that the proportion of abortions on teenage girls is lower than one might imagine. And there are more than one would think for older women who already have children, love their children, but know what it means and what it costs. This is what is so flippantly called 'convenience abortions', but it's not really like that.

Childrearing is such a huge burden that women carry and men don't in the same way. It's like a twenty-year sentence, when you're tied all the time, and once you've been through it once, you don't want to start on another twenty years.

ELAINE: And again, a woman who finds she is carrying a Downs syndrome baby in her early forties has to make a decision knowing the length of time it's going to take to look after this child. I can understand that these are very difficult decisions.

MARGARET: You would do anything to convince yourself that ending this pregnancy is not murdering a human being. And if there is even a thin thread of argument that it's not, I completely understand why women go with that.

ELAINE: But I also admire those women whose principles and commitment come together and, knowing the costs, can choose life. And I believe God honours them.

Fifteen

POST-CHRISTIANS

MARGARET: I was struck with something you said at Greenbelt which I hadn't heard before, which was that in the United States now people are using 'God' as a verb.

ELAINE: Yes, that's very common now. It started with Mary Daly twenty odd years ago in *Beyond God the Father* (Boston Beacon, 1973; Women's Press, 1985). She talks about 'verbicide', which is the murdering of the verb and replacing it by the noun. Verbicide is what men have done to God in the name of religion, and left women stranded because women need to be involved in the active, dynamic participation of God.

MARGARET: Women are more connected with verbs and men with nouns?

ELAINE: That is the idea she is positing, but it is also to do with the idea that the moment you have God as a static noun then you have conquered God, you have mastered God. When men do this then God is created in their own image, so God becomes a static patriarchal male. Therefore to deny that God is a name at all is to move towards liberation, for Mary Daly.

In *Beyond God the Father*, she rejects God the Father and also gender-neutral gods, like Power, Spirit or Force, because they are still substantive gods – names of something. She disperses with Goddess the Mother for the same reason ('The noun-goddess is a simple off-shoot of the noun-god who is a reified reversal of the ancient Verb-Goddess', p. xviii). Bit by bit she whittles all nouns away and concludes with God as a verb. But it is always the verb of being, it is 'I am', said by women coming into self-consciousness.

MARGARET: That's very Jewish, like God's 'I am who I am' in Exodus 3.

ELAINE: Yes, it is in a way. But the 'I am' is the woman speaking on behalf of herself and womankind, and collectively this 'I am' is not the Being who cannot be other than self-defined. It is the verb to be said by women.

When you come to Carter Heyward, an American Episcopalian I mentioned before, the same idea is there of God as a verb, but the verb is now 'to God'. In Heyward's lesbian theology we 'God' with one another. The pinnacle of this activity seems to be sexual godding where two women are physically wrapped up in each other.

MARGARET: Wow! I haven't read *Beyond God the Father*. I have read bits of Daly's *Gyn/Ecology* (Women's Press, 1978), and Carter Heyward I have come across in fragments. So when you God me, what are you doing to me?

ELAINE: What am I doing when I God you? I am not exploiting you, I am allowing all your freedom to flourish and blossom. I am affirming you as another human being and I am probably having a lesbian relationship with you.

The allegation made by anti-feminists is that if you start with any kind of feminism within the church you end up with Mary Daly, Carter Heyward and Daphne Hampson. It is the slippery slope argument that people like William Oddie (who has removed to your place from ours) mounted in his book *What Will Happen to God?* (SPCK, 1984). That is his argument all the way through, that if you start acknowledging that God can be spoken of without using male terms, you end up with this lot.

MARGARET: I think it is a useful book.

ELAINE: Oh, it is. I have read it over again. And we need to face the question whether post-Christian feminism leaves orthodox Christianity intact. Do we just ignore the post-Christians and write them off? Or are they saying something we need to listen to?

MARGARET: That confrontation was very vivid for me at the launch of Daphne Hampson's book *Theology and Feminism* (Blackwell, 1990). Some of my feminist friends were rather cross with what I wrote. I thought it was a terribly amusing occasion, you see, because you had the Christian feminists out in force in their dungarees and trainers and cropped hair, expecting to get words of life, and facing them was Daphne, tiny Daphne with her high heels and her big bouffant hair-style. The Christian feminists are ever hopeful, they think that a feminist is a feminist is a good thing and a feminist theologian is very much a good thing, and they found it almost inconceivable that they might not like what she said.

So there was Daphne, giving one of her lectures, which was extremely dynamic accompanied by great ordered scrawlings on the overhead projector, and she systematically

demolished Christianity, one, two, three, four, five, six. And
the Christian feminists sat there looking a little bewildered.
At question time they came back, saying, in effect, 'We
quite appreciate it is very important to say how dreadful
Christianity has been, but don't you agree it can be saved?'
And Daphne was saying 'No.'

This is where Daphne Hampson and William Oddie are in
agreement: Christianity and feminism are completely incompatible.

ELAINE: Yes, it is interesting. And John Broadhurst, a former
Anglo-Catholic spokesperson, now a bishop, says he is a
Daphne Hampson fan. I mean, I don't think he agrees with
a word she says, except for that one point. Many people want
to believe that Christianity and feminism are incompatible.

MARGARET: Daly and Hampson are the two formative influences for post-Christian feminism.

ELAINE: They are the two who call themselves post-
Christian. But as I said before, I think Carter Heyward has
a post-Christian theological position. Of course, she operates
from within the church and they can't get her out, because
she is not going! We don't have anathemas in the Anglican
communion. I heard Carter Heyward in Brazil.

MARGARET: Did you? That sort of stuff wouldn't go down
very well in Brazil, would it?

ELAINE: Well, that was interesting. It was an international
Anglican conference of two thousand people to celebrate the
Decade of Solidarity with Women. For the first three days or
so many of the addresses were about women's suffering, and

they were very poignant: accounts of incest, betrayal, prostitution, lack of understanding, all kinds of horrendous things
that women have gone through across the globe.

After that, we started to have explanations why, and Carter
Heyward's talk took on for me a rather sinister shape. It turned
out to be all the fault of Christianity, which was inevitably
patriarchal. But the effect of what she said on many of the
women was to 'liberate' them, in their words. Except for the
Africans, who really didn't like it. At one point, when somebody was talking about poor African sisters not being
ordained and so on, in a patronizing way, a Nigerian woman
shouted, 'Save your sympathy, sister, we're OK.'

After the Africans, the Brazilian women were the least
enchanted. But from other parts of the world what she was
saying got strong affirmation. I was surprised, almost alarmed,
at the response that she got.

MARGARET: That they felt liberated by her attacking
Christianity?

ELAINE: I think so, yes. Well, there had been a lot of weeping
and blood-letting and grieving, and then she came along at a
point when almost anything you said that offered a new way
of seeing things would have been helpful.

MARGARET: That links into one of the points I wanted to
make about Daly. I think the most marvellous thing about
Christianity is the recognition that the problem is my sin. But
these thinkers always blame someone else. They go so far as to
blame the male race as race.

I quite appreciate the need to reaffirm women and their
dignity, but it seems to me Daly goes too far. I do not find it
liberating, I find it imprisoning when she says, for example:

'Finally, in fairness, I thank my Self' (*Gyn/Ecology*, p. xviii). If salvation relies on my self I really am in a mess. And that line is quite strong in her writing.

ELAINE: It is her thesis from the beginning. Women are the innocents. So she takes a lot of Christian doctrine and redoes it in the light of women as the innocents who have been slaughtered in the name of God by Christians, and by Christian men.

And to the question, 'What happens when women sin? Are you really saying women are not capable of brutality or betrayal?' she concedes that some women do this, but when they do they are acting on behalf of men. Her term is that they are 'token torturers'. It is the men who somehow have so manipulated and grasped the women that the women are in bondage to these men and acting on their behalf.

Now because women are the innocents, she says they don't need to be saved from sin. The only sin is sexism, and since they are its victims women don't need to be saved from it. And that is why a male Christ can't be Saviour, because how can a male Christ save women from sexism?

MARGARET: This is so distorted.

ELAINE: It is. She slides from one distortion into another.

MARGARET: I am remembering one of the most moving liturgies I have been at. It was at Bristol during a big Christian Aid/CAFOD event for the 500th anniversary of Columbus reaching the Americas. Bristol is a lovely, beautiful city but its beauty is built on slave-money. We walked in pilgrimage through the city, looking at different sites connected with the slave trade, and at the mid-point there was a liturgy of penitence in St Stephen's Church. You heard eye-witness readings from slaves and it wrenched you apart.

The point is that it is our sin, our ancestors who did it, us who enjoy the fruits of it – even this beautiful city of Bristol. Now that sort of awareness of the sin of the past is an awareness of our complicity in it, and that is something quite different from, 'We are the innocents, they are the guilty ones.'

There are groups of people for whom that is appropriate, but that element of personal sin as well should never be lost. Apart from anything else, it is unsatisfying psychologically to offload all the blame, because the most joyous thing about Christianity is being able to say, 'I have sinned,' and to find freedom from that.

ELAINE: Yes, I agree entirely, but for Mary Daly this is what has held women down, because she argues that Christianity has laid all the sin on women, from Eve onwards. The only way to escape, she thinks, is to recognize that we are innocents, we are only sinned against.

MARGARET: I think that is wrong. I think the way to escape out of that vicious circle is to see sin in different terms. The woman who is battered by her husband, and blames herself for it, should move from seeing her sin as faults in her that provoke her husband to chastise her, to seeing her sin as her inability which may have an element of cowardice – to challenge and break free.

ELAINE: Yes, so sin can be sometimes complicity, sometimes cowardice. And sometimes it is sin against us.

MARGARET: It is not just a matter of replacing one explanation with a contrary one: 'I was to blame for this reason, now

I know it was the other one, and I am still all to blame.' But it is nonetheless an attitude of humility, isn't it? 'God, show me what I should do. I am open to you showing me the way I have behaved in the past and the way I should behave now.'

ELAINE: Yes, and it is not gender specific, that is important. Both men and women sin, even if sometimes they are guilty of different kinds of sins, as Rosemary Radford Ruether suggests. There is no way in which the whole of one sex is innocent. That makes no sense at all.

MARGARET: And Mary Daly is so provocative. I just wonder what is wrong with the woman. Her way of writing is utterly extraordinary. Listen to this: 'The Paternal Parasites hide their vampirizing of female energy by deceptive posturing, which takes the form of Processions (religious, military, judicial, academic, etc.)' (*Gyn/Ecology*, p. 30).

ELAINE: Yes, it is extraordinary. What she is doing, of course, is changing the whole nature of patriarchal writing, so she is not even buying into the thought-forms or the expressions that you get in patriarchy. So she recreates her own verbs and her own syntax, and creates long hyphenated words that put opposites together because 'liberation is the work of Wicked Grammar' (p. xxv). It is clever writing because she packs it with images, recreating her own ones in order to define the traditional images that the church has held. Somehow she speaks to people even though I find her irritating.

MARGARET: Yes, I certainly find her irritating. It is packed with invective. 'Dutifully dull and derivative, drained of divinity, she merits the reward of perpetual paralysis in patriarchal paradise' (p. 88). All that energy expended in aggression I find wearisome. And I suppose some would say it is just playing the male game again, which is the aggression game.

ELAINE: There is much muted anger there, coming out in this sophisticated linguistic idiom. There is no doubt she is brilliant with words. The demolishing and recreating of images and metaphors is very skilfully done. It is done through anger, through a deep-down, pent-up loathing of Christianity. You can hardly read any page without being clobbered by it.

MARGARET: One of the good things that she has done is to reclaim these words used of women: spinsters, lesbians, hags, harpies, crones, furies. When I was in Canada I was aware that was something quite positive: women of 65 would describe themselves as 'hags' or 'crones', turning it into a good word.

ELAINE: It is saying, 'This is what women have been called all these years within a patriarchal system. OK, if this is what we are, let's be that, let's enjoy that.'

MARGARET: But then her attack on particular Christian doctrines – it makes me despair that she can't see anything good in them.

ELAINE: Whether you are talking about the annunciation, or the Second Coming, or anything Christological, they are women-denying for her and have to be redone. But redoing them involves the annunciation becoming a cosmic rape scene.

MARGARET: I have a quote on that: 'In the charming story of "the Annunciation" the angel Gabriel appears to the terrified young girl, announcing that she has been chosen to become the mother of god. Her response to this sudden proposal from the godfather is totaled nonresistance: "Let it be done unto me according to thy word." Physical rape is not necessary when the mind/will/spirit has already been invaded' (*ibid.*, p. 85).

So there is that precious moment in Christianity – the archetype of us saying 'Yes' to God – and she can't see anything good in it.

ELAINE: Using the godfather image – like a tyrannical, patriarchal Mafia boss who can take what he wants from anyone – fuses the idea of the Godhead with violence and corruption.

MARGARET: And then how can anyone speak of 'the dreary dogma of "resurrection from the dead" ' (p. 101)? Easter energizes, inspires people. How can she write it off as a dreary dogma? I don't know what in her history makes her feel this way.

ELAINE: Her history is that she was a Catholic theologian in Boston College and she preached a sermon about the exodus community, where she said in effect, 'Singing sexist hymns, praying to a male God, crushes our spirit, so let's affirm our sisterhood by rising and walking out together.' And apparently when she left the chapel, most others left with her.

That was the beginning of the end. That sermon is a passionate and sad and very dispirited plea to other women. I have the text and it is in quite normal language. It is not like the stuff becomes later. In her experiences in the theological faculty and the Catholic Church, she had already rocked the boat a good deal. And then this stuff bubbled up inside and she quit the church.

MARGARET: It is very much an anti-Catholic thing, then?

ELAINE: Oh, it was very much an anti-Catholic thing. It wasn't that she was excusing Protestants, she just wasn't that familiar with Protestantism.

MARGARET: But the oppression of women is much worse in Catholicism, at least in terms of what you are allowed to do.

ELAINE: Daphne Hampson's journey also begins with what she perceives as rejection by the church. There is no other avenue of expressing this sense of rejection other than by quitting and making a big scene. That is what they do.

MARGARET: But Daphne Hampson does it completely differently, doesn't she? She is so cool, so fiercely intellectual and so cerebral.

ELAINE: That is what makes it very interesting: that you get two post-Christian feminists who probably agree a great deal in terms of the diagnosis of what is wrong with the church, but who represent two completely different strands, not only of church background but also of philosophy.

Daphne Hampson's arguments against Christianity are in the end Enlightenment arguments, she hasn't moved into the postmodern era at all. Her arguments are based on the rational noncomprehensiveness of the church and its inability to answer some fundamental questions. Even the way she couches the sexism is in post-Enlightenment phrases and arguments. Everything that David Hume and other sceptics and atheists were raking over at the Enlightenment – that is where she is.

Now if you look at Mary Daly she is light years away from the Enlightenment. She is not interested in debate, she is interested in weaving these wonderful images and doing things with words that express the way she feels. She is not didactic and argumentative, not mounting a thesis or demolishing somebody else's thesis. She does it in a very different way, in a verbal context.

So the two are very different. Daphne Hampson represents something idiosyncratically Scottish, and Mary Daly something very American. But also they are poles apart in terms of which era they belong to.

MARGARET: When you say Daphne Hampson is not at all postmodern, can you spell that out a little more?

ELAINE: Postmodernity invites us to turn our back on the past and recreate reality in the present. We can choose whichever reality we wish to create, which is what Mary Daly is doing all the time with her words – recreating a reality different from that which is presented by Christianity by, for example, saying the annunciation is a cosmic rape scene. She creates a different way of seeing things in antipathy to the church.

There is a kind of smorgasbord mentality: you take your plate along and you fill it with whatever goods you want. It doesn't matter if they don't taste the same or go together, you can change them into whatever you want. Mary Daly does that with her post-Christian theology. She is putting all kinds of things together that we might think don't fit, but she likes them that way.

Daphne Hampson, on the other hand, is rigorous, systematic and structural and would not put together things that don't belong, because there is something intellectually dissatisfying about that. But it is interesting that when you put those two traditions together they mount a formidable attack on Christianity. Just as you think you have answered Daphne Hampson, Mary Daly clobbers you from a very different perspective.

MARGARET: Going on to Daphne's rejection by the church, what you say is absolutely right and is the first thing you read in her book *Theology and Feminism* (1990) She says that she had wished for twenty years to be ordained, and that is a long time. 'Eleven years ago [this book was published in 1990], it was I who wrote the statement in favour of the ordination of women to the priesthood circulated to all members of the General Synod of the Church of England before the vote. Today finds me no longer Christian' (p. 4).

I don't know who first coined the word post-Christian...

ELAINE: I think it was said about Mary Daly.

MARGARET: ...well, Daphne says, 'I am post-Christian. Post-Christian because Christianity (and not Islam) is the historical context within which my religious sensibilities were formed. But definitely post-Christian because I do not believe that there could be this uniqueness: that God could be related in a particular way to a particular age or to one particular person, Jesus Christ' (p. 42). And there is a rather nice image: 'an observant friend once remarked that whereas Christian feminists want to change the actors in the play, what I want is a different kind of play' (p. 162).

Daphne's main challenge is to the idea of Christians having a historical particularity. 'I do not believe, whatever I may mean by God, that it could be said of God that God was differently related to one age or people than God is related to all ages or people. God is something which is always available' p. 8).

I don't find her challenge convincing, because if you are going to make God equally available all the time, God disappears in the process. For God to have meaning you have to be able to say, 'Here are graced moments, here are graced situations, here are graced people.' And if God speaks more through some people than through others, God speaks most of all through Christ. I don't find that an intellectual difficulty.

ELAINE: We need to stress that, because she comes back to that point over and over again. The fact that she is not a Christian is only to do with her feminism at a second point; the first point is to do with the particularity of Christ. Whereas for Mary Daly it is all to do with what the church has done to women. But for Daphne Hampson it is an intellectual problem.

MARGARET: I think the reason why people flock to hear her talk is in the final paragraph of the book, which does sound a lot of chords: 'Many a woman – in a way in which this has not on the whole been true of men – has had to turn her back upon the religion within which she grew up. It simply became impossible. For any woman apprised of what the history of women has been, the question of theodicy raised by the previous conception of God has made that conception of God unthinkable' (p. 173). There is a lot of pain there, which other people share.

ELAINE: You can't be with Daphne Hampson for more than a few minutes without experiencing the pain. I think it is even more true when she meets a woman who is still a Christian but at the same time sympathetic to feminism. The pain comes out very sharply indeed.

I have met her on several occasions; we debated at Greenbelt and did a radio programme for Norwegian Radio.

I found myself quite drawn to her as a person. But she can be quite strong also in her rejection of Christianity. It is interesting that she has found a niche in a Quaker environment.

MARGARET: She is very much a believer in worship. She never misses a Sunday. That's what she told me a few years ago when I went up to St Andrews. She said: 'I never miss a week.' And she gave a talk on prayer which I heard.

ELAINE: To whom does she pray?

MARGARET: She does believe in God but not in the Christian conception of God. I don't know what words she uses. But she does pray.

And then I heard her say in a lecture once that the point came in reading the Bible when she couldn't bear to open it any more, she just found it too painful. And that was just a little glimpse of what is going on behind it all.

ELAINE: That comes out in the book you referred to. In one long section entitled 'Angst, Death and Eternal Life' (pp. 137–42) she is arguing that much of theology is in tune with the male psyche and out of tune with the female psyche. Here she moves into the area of big generalizations.

She takes a concept like angst, anxiety without an object, and claims that it is predominantly men who suffer from this foreboding feeling. She says it feeds into the idea of the sinner standing before the face of a wrathful God, just on his own. She says this is an idea much more central for men than women, because it is closer to their psychological make-up. But because of their 'connectedness' women don't experience anxiety without an object; we have anxiety about real people and real events.

She does the same with the notion of life after death, showing how it relates to men's sense of individuality and separateness, so they need to have something of themselves to survive. She argues that women are less interested in life after death than life in the now, the present; they survive anyway by giving birth to children.

Now, when I went over this with my philosophy class, they were infuriated. I had set her book as a normal text in philosophy and religion and I was surprised by the negative reaction. Both men and women felt they had been stereotyped. One man insisted that he didn't have this angst, whereas one of the women said she did, but didn't experience 'connectedness'. So that was quite interesting.

MARGARET: I react rather like your students. I dislike intensely theories that say men are like this, women are like that, because I feel imprisoned by that and I want to say, 'No, a large part of me is like what you say is male, and I don't want that labelled as my "animus", thanks very much, because why should I have bits of me labelled as the male bits as though they are somehow less mine than the female bits?'

I notice Daphne uses those terms: 'Our anima must complement our animus' (p. 4). I am surprised, because the feminists I know are all very anti-Jungian, in the way I am. They hate this talk of 'anima' and 'animus'.

Something else which I would want to dispute is that for her 'the present is normative and the past is only drawn upon in so far as that seems to be appropriate' (p. 11). Now why should the present be normative? Why should we be right today and everyone in the past be wrong? The present cannot have a sort of priority because it is the present.

In relation to particular questions – feminism is one of those questions, and slavery another – one can be so confident that the past was wrong that one can have confidence in the right insight of the present. But that is not because it is the insight of the present day, it is because of the strength of the conviction.

ELAINE: The idea that only the present matters doesn't begin to make sense to me, because what is the present other than that which has grown out of the past? So yes, we have more problems now about the environment and ecology, because we are in a different century. But Christianity has spoken about the environment and ecology right from the very beginning. We have discovered it now, but it has always been there.

I think that Christian truth has always been against slavery but they didn't face it fully until a hundred and fifty years ago. I think Christianity has always been for equality for women, but we are only beginning to move into that in a full way.

MARGARET: This is a very interesting discussion, and I want to say two things. One is that the priority of the present is linked to the priority of the self. Remember Daly's 'I thank my Self'? It is a little bit the same in Hampson, that the way I see things today is right.

Now obviously we think we are right because if we didn't think we were right we wouldn't hold that view. But what is so precious in Christianity – and this is particularly a Catholic approach, though not exclusively so – is the sense of humility vis-à-vis the teaching of the church. 'It may seem this way to me, but who am I to know? So I am not going to put my personal opinion up above the wisdom of the church.'

That seems to me a fundamental act of humility that is intellectually completely cogent as well as psychologically appropriate. So the feminism of Hampson and that of Daly has a bit too much self in it. 'I am the measure of all things, I determine truth.'

If you take the fundamental tenet of feminism to be the equality of women and men – rather than the superiority of women – then where can that be found more strongly than in the Judaeo-Christian revelation of human equality before God? And in the incarnation, where it was human nature that God took on? And in the idea that in death our bodies turn to dust, and we are all on the same level facing our Maker, with no hierarchy of race or social position? That is where we learn these values.

ELAINE: Daphne Hampson's critique is of individual survival after death, which she sees as a male preoccupation, but she does not focus on death as the leveller, death as that which reduces all of us to the same standing, whether we are Pope, or women who scrub the lavatories all their lives.

Sixteen

WORSHIP

♀ MARGARET: Liturgy has been a very painful area for me, and there are different strategies – not all successful – for dealing with it. Some of them are negative in that a lot of the time when I go to church I just feel detached from it.

ELAINE: Let's talk about the pain first of all. You've already said it's not because of the male Christ? So is it the priest?

MARGARET: It's the priest. Not the fact that the priest is a man, but the fact that the priest has to be a man.

ELAINE: All right. And is the pain specific to the Eucharist or is it in any church service?

MARGARET: It could be in any. But it's essentially connected with the Eucharist because of the particular ban in the Catholic Church on women presiding. I mean, we hardly ever have a service which is not a Eucharist.

ELAINE: Of course.

MARGARET: So if I go to another one, it's for an ecumenical occasion, and then that's usually more creative anyway. So it's not usually painful. Very occasionally we have a service which is not a Mass. I went to one in Advent and it was irritating because the priest-chaplain did it, but it was the one service in the whole year that the woman chaplain who is not a priest could have done. Not that he didn't do it well, but it was a missed opportunity.

ELAINE: I think your pain is bound to be more intense than my pain because although the Eucharist is very important, it is only one of our many opportunities to worship together.

MARGARET: It's taken a while for that pain to grow. There was a stage when I would feel pain at the Eucharist, but not necessarily because of the women question. For example, one of the things that always causes me pain is when we don't have the Eucharist under both kinds, we just have the host. That was the old-fashioned Catholic practice. And of course it's completely contrary to what Jesus said at the Last Supper, which is 'Drink from it, all of you' (Matthew 26:27).

ELAINE: Of course, yes. I've never ever understood the Catholic practice on that. I just assumed there's some reason that's beyond me!

MARGARET: I can't remember what the reason is but I think it was historical, not theological. But there is a theological reason for why it doesn't matter, which is that under each kind you receive Christ whole and entire so you don't have to have both. But the sign value is fuller under both kinds.

I resent that exclusion enormously, and I got to the point where I'd write little letters to parish priests. But then I found even if that bit was right there was still pain, and so much else wrong, and the women question is the worst thing of all. Absolutely the worst thing of all.

One thing I do is just go and feel the pain, that's what I probably do most of the time. However, I have been at Catholic Masses where I've been completely happy, and there are two ways in which that can happen. One is if it's in a context in which other meanings are so important that the women issue fades into insignificance. I've felt that in the third world: if I'm with some peasants up a hillside in Nicaragua then I'm really not going to be bothered about the sexism, because there's so much else that the Eucharist is consoling them for and it's wonderful to feel I'm in one communion with them.

And just at the moment I'm finding it less painful than I did in the past because I'm very conscious of the Eucharist as a means of communion with Peter, a sharing in the heavenly banquet. That's highlighted a new emphasis which means that the sexism just recedes into the background.

So that's one way in which the pain goes, and another is when people use every possible opportunity within the Mass to make feminist points, which makes it sound rather political but actually I find it very healing. There are all sorts of things that can be done. For example, at a retreat I went to last November three out of four of the retreat team were women, and for the daily Mass they took it in turns to do the liturgy of the Word. And even when the priest took over, he took over in the most humble possible way, sitting round at different points around the circle on different days with a tiny little table in front of him.

And throughout the week he used a series of different Trinitarian formulae, none of which was Father, Son and Spirit.

ELAINE: Really?

MARGARET: Yes. They were all inclusive and for me it was marvellous, it was a symbol, and a constant reminder and a token. Shelter, Shepherd, Sustainer. There was something new to think about each day. Listener, Liberator, Life-giver. Each of them, of course, is theologically inadequate taken on its own, but then Father, Son and Spirit is also theologically inadequate in a different kind of way. It was a way of rounding the thing, another little crumb to make up the total picture. These are just little things which are probably breaking the rules – in fact I'm sure they are breaking the rules – but they say so much to me.

I was even at a Mass once – I will definitely not say where or in what circumstances it was, or I'll get them into terrible trouble – when the entire Eucharistic prayer was read by a woman and she stopped at the point: 'he broke the bread and gave it to his disciples saying', and then the priest said the actual words of consecration, 'Take this, all of you, and eat it, this is my body.'

ELAINE: Very imaginative.

MARGARET: It was. Very dramatic, and it felt very good.

ELAINE: That's tremendous.

MARGARET: So if there is some sign from the priest or the people organizing the liturgy that they recognize the problem, that's enough for me to feel included and reconciled with that community.

ELAINE: For me, I think, it has always been more liberating when a woman preaches than when she administers communion, because I have regularly experienced the administration of women at communion, especially in many of the Free churches where I have sometimes worshipped. In Anglican churches women have been involved in the administration of the wine for as long as I can remember. But they have always been less likely to preach. It is just regarded as much more of a man's thing.

In the eighties when we used to have our early women's conferences, we always had a liturgy-writing workshop which wrote something for the end of the day that we could all use together as an act of common worship. What was beautiful was that women who chose that workshop had often been quite powerfully hurt by liturgy and felt excluded from it, whether it was within the Church of England or another church. Once they had shared that with the group, they learnt to work through it into something much more constructive that they could bring to all of us to be used.

And I remember one of them rewrote the sections of the reminder of the great cloud of witnesses (Hebrews 11) where we remember the patriarchs, and instead they remembered the patriarch's wives – Sarah and Rebecca and Leah and Rachel – and the women of faith – Miriam and Deborah – and that had a wonderful kind of healing in it. There was so much that came out of those liturgy-writing workshops.

In many Anglican churches, I would say for the last fifteen if not twenty years, the services have been very inclusive in the sense that everybody takes some part: the laity, the ordained clergy, children, families, old people. In some churches, the Eucharistic prayers are read by the congregation as a whole. In the absolution some of the ministers – the men, before the ordination of women – would use the inclusive 'us' rather than 'you', to make a point, I suppose, that the clergy need to receive absolution as much as to give it.

What stands out is that, given all the other changes in worship, this one symbolic act of communion stretches right back through the centuries to the first followers of Christ, and that seems to be so much more significant than whoever administers it. I remember the first time I administered the bread – it must have been about fifteen years ago. The minister in whose church I was preaching just handed it to me and said, 'You will administer the bread and I the wine,' which struck me as incredibly audacious and radical but I did it. But afterwards I thought, 'I've never done that before,' and I asked him and he said, 'It's quite normal practice for whoever preaches, but we don't always have women preaching, obviously.'

The pain in the Anglican Church has been felt far more acutely when women ordained as deacons were not allowed to preside at the Eucharist. Women who felt called to a priestly role would often say they were allowed to be priestly in all other areas except this one. I understood that but didn't feel that way myself because my experience is different.

MARGARET: But that is also what forced the change, isn't it? Because people felt this is so ridiculous.

ELAINE: Yes, quite, and it was ridiculous, really, because women were doing everything else and it made the priesthood into some magical thing in a way that Anglicans have never believed it to be. It recalled an idea about priesthood which has never really been Anglican. I'm not sure how authentically Catholic it is, either.

MARGARET: Meaning?

ELAINE: The confusion between the priest being a representation of Christ rather than the representative of Christ. Being a representation meant you had to look like Christ: i.e. be male. That is not an Anglican position, but it seemed to be the only grounds on which you could exclude women if they were doing everything else.

MARGARET: It's a good distinction which I have never actually heard before. I don't think we do hold that officially, but you get flashes of it. You saw it rearing its head when Ann Widdecombe was saying a woman priest would be like having a man play the Virgin Mary. Which actually one would not mind at all, because there are theatre companies that have all male actors playing female roles and there is no problem. I saw a fantastic *As You Like It* by the Cheek by Jowl Company that did just that.

ELAINE: Can I just ask another point, because I'm still quite dense on this. What part do women play in the Eucharist in the Catholic Church, or what part may they play? What are you laughing at?

MARGARET: They can sit in the pew and kneel in the pew and stand up in the pew, and they can read the responses. They can always do that.

But in most churches – not every church – they can give out the elements, if they are Eucharistic ministers. That's a very simple procedure, often no more than a day of talks. The parish priest invites you and then the bishop says some words over everyone all together. It's terribly straightforward and easy.

At first it was very good because women were doing more, but then, after it had been going on for a few years, the fact that that's all they're allowed to do makes it even more painful. It draws attention to the fact that they can go no further.

There's one church where I go sometimes where women don't do anything. They don't take the collection, they don't take part in the offertory procession, they don't act as servers, they are just not visible in any liturgical act. I think they can read, but that's all. And in some ways that's less painful because it doesn't keep on rubbing your nose into the fact that you have token women doing menial jobs. In some ways it's more satisfactory not to see them at all.

So it's a very difficult issue, and how do you cope? Do you cope with having them doing as much as they're allowed? Or do you avoid going to Mass? Or do you say the Eucharist is too important to let this worry me? The Eucharist has enormously important meanings which are nothing to do with this, and sometimes one can forget about the problems. It just depends on what moment in my life I'm at.

Sometimes I've felt that Catholics found it easier to accept women administering communion than a lot of Anglicans.

ELAINE: Oh, right?

MARGARET: Because for Protestants the holy sacramental thing is in the administration, isn't it? You have this idea that what isn't used of the bread you can take and use in your kitchen or give to the birds, which is very shocking to Catholics. For Protestants the bread becomes the body of Christ in the act of giving and receiving it, with those words and with that intention. Whereas Catholics have located the holiness in the act of consecration.

So we have actually been very happy about women administering communion, and when the laity began to do that after the Council there was no theological reason to make a fuss. There still are some people who would prefer to go to a priest, but very few, and on the whole the congregations are completely used to women administering either the chalice or the host. I have noticed some of my Protestant friends weren't quite as happy about it as we were, because of that act itself being more endued with meaning. Is that fair?

ELAINE: Yes, that's quite true. It's of a piece for Anglicans, and always has been, with the prayers. So for some Anglicans, when you open the administration to women, why don't you open everything else? What is the big deal?

MARGARET: I'll say something about other strategies for coping with sexist liturgy. At ordination services in the USA – I don't know whether they are doing this at the moment but I have heard of it in the past – people have worn a black armband, even ordinands, and then the bishop has been reluctant to ordain them with it on and they have had to cover it up, which has been farcical. It is difficult to know, isn't it, when it is appropriate to have a demo in the course of a liturgy?

In Holy Week there was a demo outside Westminster Cathedral at the chrism Mass, when all the priests of the diocese come. I wasn't there. Demonstrating at a liturgy is difficult, maybe that is why I didn't go. I supported it in theory and maybe I just chickened out. One doesn't like to make a bad atmosphere.

ELAINE: No.

MARGARET: What do you feel about demos in churches, and outside churches?

ELAINE: I don't like them in churches. If it's worship, the whole point of worship is to be reconciled to God and to leave your disagreements at the door, and that is far more important than anything else. That is why I have put up with all kinds of nonsense within a worship service, that afterwards I have exploded about. But while it is on I have resisted walking out of the church or making any kind of protest even when I have heard horrible things from the pulpit and wanted to bolt. I may have found it impossible to worship, but other people haven't, so you have to respect that.

I have left early on a couple of occasions, when the offending thing was over, because it seemed meaningless to stay, but I've left in quietness, looking as though I ought to be making the dinner or something, not with a big fuss or demonstration. I can't see myself ever actually stomping out of something, because of the hurt it would cause. There have to be other strategies for dealing with it.

But it is different where you are making a point strongly but still worshipping inclusively with other people. Maybe the wearing of the armband comes into that category: saying something, but not disturbing the flow of worship, and still with people you disagree with in an act which is about reconciliation.

MARGARET: I have often felt, going up to communion, that I would like a badge or something to distance me from this act even as I do it. Yet at the same time I don't want to do that because of what you say.

ELAINE: Oddly enough, the only communion that I have never been able to take in my whole life was at the post-Christian feminist conference, where we were praying to the west winds and the mother earth and covering ourselves with sweetgrasses and taking the body of God of Christa. That is the only time I couldn't actually do it. Isn't that extraordinary?

MARGARET: Do I know of this conference?

ELAINE: It was at an international Anglican conference in Brazil, They had rewritten all the liturgies, which was fine, better in many ways. But a group of North American feminists pushed us too far, and when it came to the Eucharist I felt what was happening was pagan. It was a very difficult decision whether I participated or not, whether to show solidarity with all these women or stand out on my own. I decided not to take communion, and then to my enormous relief I saw rows and rows of African women from different countries also sitting absolutely static. One of them told me afterwards, 'This is what we were liberated from in Africa and we are not going back to it.'

MARGARET: Was it billed as post-Christian?

ELAINE: No, and it wasn't. It was a very fine conference until towards the end when it became evident that a bunch of American feminists with a strong agenda were steering things. They did it in the name of inclusivism. It was interesting that some of the Brazilians as well as the Africans said, 'This does not include us, sisters, we feel outside.' Coping with that Eucharist was far more painful than coping with all the ones I was used to for decades.

MARGARET: One tiny gesture, which I found meant a lot to me when I was in Canada at a university chaplaincy, was that the first person to speak at the Mass was a woman. She was the leader of the musicians and she just said something simple like, 'I welcome you all to our Eucharist today and we will begin by singing hymn number whatever.' It bracketed everything else. It was presiding over the presider really. And that, of course, is legitimate.

ELAINE: Yes, that's lovely.

MARGARET: One strategy that I haven't mentioned is that of not going to Mass but going to something else. I have heard dramatic statistics about the numbers of women religious superiors who don't go regularly to Mass any more, for precisely this reason.

In Oxford there is a Christian women's liturgy group that meets monthly and is ecumenical. It doesn't celebrate the Eucharist, but sometimes it celebrates *agapes*. For a lot of people that is the Eucharist, so I prefer to go when it is something completely different.

Sometimes I choose to go to that rather than to Mass: I suppose I go a couple of times a year. And if I have a particular reason for going to an Anglican service, then I don't usually go to Mass as well. The rule I give myself is to worship with a Christian community of some sort at least once a week.

So I tend to take opportunities to escape going to Mass, and the reason is because it's sexist. It's a shame, because I would like to pray with the other people. It's always a dilemma.

What do you feel about women-only liturgies?

ELAINE: Oh, I enjoy them. It is a time when women can experience their womanliness in relation to each other, and there is a lot of sharing. I find them quite emotional.

I have led a number of women's retreats, for women ordained and lay (including women in religious orders). And what brings us together is that we are Christian women, not that we are ordained or religious or whatever. It is that sense of understanding one another's lives, and although we normally ask an ordained woman to lead the communion, it does not actually matter much who presides. There is a sense of inclusiveness there.

There are a number of liturgies for women gathering together in those sorts of situations and they are lovely, I like them very much. When women gather together as women, and there is a feminist agenda by being there, it is wonderful. But when women gather together as feminists it is different.

MARGARET: Yes, that is true, isn't it?

ELAINE: So I think strategies for me have been easier, because there are a lot of options, and because I love the Eucharist as the key symbolic act which stretches back to the time that Jesus was here with his disciples.

MARGARET: But that is precisely where the pain is, that this is so important and it is so spoilt. If only it wasn't this wonderful act that stretches back to Jesus I wouldn't mind so much.

I don't know if I told you of the retreat I went on, not the most recent one but the one before, when by my own choice I did not receive any sacraments. And this was even though I happened to have chosen a priest, a man, to be my spiritual director. So I did not go to confession – the sacrament of reconciliation. Well, in fact I went to a woman, which was non-sacramental. That was my decision: I wanted to overcome any barrier in myself to going to a woman.

And I didn't go to Mass all week. I'm not sure my director understood that, but for me it was an important and precious decision that I had been able, as a matter of personal integrity, to say, 'I am not happy about receiving sacraments on these conditions, and I would rather trust in God and do without.'

There are some wonderful words by Mary Ward, in the seventeenth century, when she was confronted with conditions for lifting her excommunication that went against her conscience. She said, 'I will cast myself rather on the mercy of Jesus Christ and die without the sacraments.' To receive communion is to make an act of endorsement of what is going on, and in that sense I think there is always an element of objective sin in accepting the Catholic sacrament, even alongside all the good reasons for going to communion that make it a holy thing to do.

Now, in practice, on all sorts of occasions I may feel that, but I will also feel that I should join in, for the sake of the other people. The beautiful thing about an individually directed retreat is the utter selfishness of it. You can do what's best for you. But in a community a lot of people would not understand if I stopped going to communion.

ELAINE: Of course.

MARGARET: But I felt I had done something personally valuable when for one week I had sought intimacy with God in the closest possible way, and had trusted in God rather than compromising my beliefs.

ELAINE: Yes, I understand that. When I go to Anglo-Catholic churches I feel very similar. I enjoy Anglo-Catholic worship for a range of reasons, but I don't always feel comfortable at the Eucharist, because of the male monopoly. There are so many men doing these holy things and it feels almost paternalist for women to receive the truth only from men. It is disenfranchising at a very fundamental level.

Sometimes it strikes me at big diocesan conferences where I have been speaking. After a wonderfully liberating weekend, suddenly on the Sunday we go to communion and it's almost like business as usual. Many bishops are not like that but attempt to incorporate into the Eucharist what has been happening all weekend. But when it doesn't happen, I wonder what has got through from the last few days. It can be saddening when you and others have shared so much so people know what the issues are, and there is still a level of sensitivity there that is missing.

So I suppose it matters to me more than I realize, if I stop and think about it. It's just that week by week there isn't a problem for me. In the churches I belong to there is much more a sense of sharing, so it is not just the communion but actually the fellowship of believers around the Eucharist that matters. When you are handed the cup, a word of encouragement or blessing, or even your name, is given and that means a lot to me.

A few weeks ago I was visiting a church with a woman priest whom I know well in team ministry. She put her hand on my shoulder, handed me the chalice and said, 'My dear Elaine, bless you,' and then gave me the Eucharistic words. I was feeling particularly tired and low and that was a double blessing, the blessing of the Eucharist but also this priestly and loving act of communion between the two of us. Women are particularly good at that, I find.

I don't know how that is in the Catholic Church.

MARGARET: Under this Pope there has been such a tightening up, doing everything by the rules, not straying from the book by one word. But those things do mean a lot, I agree, and sometimes it can be done. I remember, in a very small group Mass, when the priest poured the drop of water into the wine he invited us all to pour a drop in, and to say our names, so our names went into the wine that became the blood of Christ, and that was beautiful. That was just one little imaginative thing.

ELAINE: That's lovely.

MARGARET: I mean, if that was institutionalized, if it was done at every Mass, it could become ritualistic again.

ELAINE: Sure.

MARGARET: So you have to have a bit of variety.

ELAINE: I had a lovely experience recently at a big youth conference, Soul Survivor, where I'd been participating. I'd been team-teaching with my youngest son, Caleb, in one seminar, which in itself was a hilariously wonderful experience. We loved it, and it worked very well indeed. (We'd done a whole session on 'Your stress is killing me', where we'd talked about domestic stress and parent–child problems, and looked at households which maximize stress, and how one deals with it in an effective Christian way. We acted it out at the beginning and it was very funny.)

Anyway, at the end of the week we had the Eucharist. The convenors of the conference had prayed about this beforehand and selected a number of presidents. There were, I think, five people who presided, three men and two women, because it was a huge gathering of about six thousand people. So I was one of the presidents and each of us chose two people to help us with the administration, and I was expecting Alan and Caleb to be with me to administer.

The hall was huge and it was grouped off into areas, and the presidents prayed the liturgical prayer as a whole.

MARGARET: Simultaneously?

ELAINE: Yes, simultaneously.

MARGARET: So there were ordained people praying?

ELAINE: Ordained and non-ordained. In fact, there was a bishop as one of the presidents.

And then the invitation was given for the other administrators to come up, and for people to take communion. Alan was there, but Caleb had disappeared, he was praying with someone. So I looked around to choose someone to help. Normally you would never do that on the spot. But I just had this sense about this lass I'd been watching, who was so caught up in worship, it was wonderful to be near her. She was obviously experiencing God in a powerful and personal way. So I quietly went over to her and I explained that I was going to preside at the communion in this area, and would she help. She looked neither surprised nor thrown, but just looked up and said, 'Oh yes,' and followed me to the front.

I gave her the elements, and in a perfectly dignified way, as though she'd been doing it all her life, she gave the cup to those who came. The three of us worked together so well and it really felt that we were God's vehicle of communion for those people. Often there was a sense of the sheer need of people who were coming, knowing they were welcomed by the Christ who had died for them. At the end we administered the sacraments to each other and prayed together and there was a deep bonding between the three of us. I'd never seen this girl before, and I've not seen her since, but something to do with the body of Christ through the ages communicated itself so strongly between us.

MARGARET: A young girl?

ELAINE: A young girl of maybe 20. But it was that simple 'Oh yes,' and the way she got up and followed me without embarrassment or giddiness or giggles, but total dignity and reverence, just as though this had been her whole life's calling.

For me that has stayed as a very special thing, that if women are not made to feel that they're weird and doing something that's completely wrong in the Eucharistic act, the dignity just comes.

CLOSING PRAYER

MARGARET: It has been a long time, a time of friendship growing as well as thoughts being woven.

ELAINE: I can't say how much I've enjoyed these conversations. It feels funny to have come to the end of the book and to be ready to launch it out. I think it would be good to commit the book to God in prayer.

MARGARET: Yes, let's do that.

God, our living love, we come to you with all our uncertainties and our searchings, and with the desire to know you truly as you really are.

We come to you with the difficulties we have known in our lives, some of which – not all – have been connected to being a woman today.

We come to you with our love of so many other women around the world who are suffering: those suffering genital mutilation, those tied to a constant pattern of exhausting childbearing and childrearing, those lacking financial freedom or the right to own land, those lacking a culture in which a woman can act on her own independently.

We come to you with the pain that is shared by so many woman around the world: believing that our womanhood is something you have given us as a strength, and yet experiencing it as a reason for discrimination.

We come to you with the belief that you bring our womanhood to fulfilment, and that in following you, Jesus, there is no incompatibility between our commitment to women and our commitment to you.

Lead us into the exciting future in which, with the help of women's understanding, we will come to know and understand you better.

ELAINE: God our Creator, our Saviour, our Friend, we come to you with both joy and petition, as Margaret has prayed, for so many women worldwide who do not share our lives of comfort. We cry to you for their help. We pray that you will move the hearts of politicians, decision-makers and people within the church, to release those who are captive to systems of cruelty, of consumerism, of prostitution, of menacing ways. We thank you that we can come to someone who understands and who knows, and whose heart is for women.

And as we pray for these, we pray also for those who will be reading this book. Bless them as they come to these final pages. We pray for whatever condition they are in, whatever history is theirs, whatever background they come from, whatever present struggles they face, and we ask that you will give them peace. We pray that your liberating Father-Mother love will soak into their lives and their hearts so that they might know that they are free in you.

And so we close our time together in these conversations and leave this in your hands, asking for your blessing in the name of Jesus our Saviour. Amen.

Also available in Fount Paperbacks

Magnify the Lord

A devotional reading of Mary's Song

Elaine Storkey

Mary's song of praise anticipating the birth of Christ is one of the most beautiful and expressive parts of the Bible. Elaine Storkey's original study of the much-loved words of the Magnificat explores its relevance for today. The timeless concerns of homes and homelessness, birth and renewal, family and the search for happiness are all seen in the light of Mary's moving response to the promise of God's faithfulness.

Each concise chapter is followed by questions and a prayer, making this inspiring book an ideal companion for personal reflection or group use.

'Lucidity, realism and a certain heart-warming quality'
Church Times

Way of St Ignatius

Finding God in all things

Margaret Hebblethwaite

The living tradition of prayer stemming from Ignatius, the sixteenth-century founder of the Jesuits, is still increasing in popularity among Christians of all denominations today. It leads us, not away from the world, but into the heart of the world where God can be found in all things.

Widely praised as one of the best introductions to the Spiritual Exercises of St Ignatius, this book combines sound practical advice on how to set about praying with an understanding of the deep mystery and beauty of prayer. 'Ignatian spirituality is about discovering the unique person that each of us is, the individual ways in which each of us relates to God, and the unprescribable ways in which we are each called to do God's will.'

> '...tackles the spiritual exercises in a forthright but sensitive way ... an imaginative approach to a deeper understanding and love of God.'
>
> *The Universe*

> 'This is an excellent, very readable and practical guide to the spiritual exercises of St Ignatius Loyola, showing clearly their earthiness, sublimity and relevance to every aspect of human life.'
>
> *Gerard W Hughes SJ*